DOES THAT MAKE SENSE?

DOES THAT MAKE SENSE?

THE BEST OF JOE BLUNDO

Joe Blundo

with a Foreword by Ted Decker

TRILLIUM, AN IMPRINT OF
THE OHIO STATE UNIVERSITY PRESS
COLUMBUS

Published by Trillium, an imprint of The Ohio State University Press.

Library of Congress Cataloging-in-Publication Data
Names: Blundo, Joe, 1954– author. | Decker, Ted (Theodore), writer of foreword.
Title: Does that make sense? : the best of Joe Blundo / Joe Blundo ; with a foreword by Ted Decker.
Other titles: Columbus dispatch (Newspaper)
Description: Columbus : Trillium, an imprint of The Ohio State University Press, [2019]
Identifiers: LCCN 2018054861 | ISBN 9780814255315 (paperback : alk. paper)
Subjects: LCSH: American newspapers—Sections, columns, etc. | American wit and humor.
Classification: LCC PS3602.L8835 A6 2019 | DDC 814/.6—dc23
LC record available at https://lccn.loc.gov/2018054861

Cover design by 4EyesDesign
Text design by Juliet Williams
Type set in Adobe Palatino

♾ The paper used in this publication meets the minimum requirements of the American National Standard for Information Sciences—Permanence of Paper for Printed Library Materials. ANSI Z39.48-1992.

CONTENTS

FOREWORD

If you're holding this book, chances are you already know about Joe Blundo's wry humor, his twisted wit, and his knack for finding stories in everyday events that—to the rest of us—wouldn't even register as events. Unless you're a writer, you might miss another of his strengths. Three times a week, I marvel at Joe's ability to say so much in so few words.

Back when I was just getting started as a newspaperman, an editor imparted a bit of print journalism truth that has stayed with me for a quarter-century. In newspapers of yore—a time not so long ago but before the wild and wooly Internet threw print journalism into its nail-biting identity crisis—the biggest commodity was space. There is only so much editorial real estate in a printed newspaper. We call that the newshole—the empty space that remains once those money-making display ads are on the pages.

That space is measured in column inches, and reporters still fight hard for their share of it. Every day is a push-and-pull between reporters who insist they cannot properly tell their tale in under 20 inches, and editors who know that any writer worth a damn could do it in 10. I was engaged in just such an argument when my editor put me in my place. "The only stories worth 18 inches," he said, "are the Second Coming and a good fishing feature." A bit of hyperbole, perhaps, with truth at its core. Stories don't have to be long to be good. And in a related bit of wisdom often misattributed to Mark Twain, it is much harder to write short than long.

That's what strikes me about Joe's columns. He illuminates life's littlest absurdities but also its greatest joys and griefs, and he does it in half the words it would take other writers. If the writing game were *Name That Tune,* Joe would be a returning champion:

I can tell that story in 500 words.
Joe Blundo, tell that story!

If you don't write, this may not seem significant. Trust me, it is. Consider that the end of this paragraph brings this foreword to nearly 400 words. In this space Joe can tickle your ribs, illuminate your life, and break your heart. Who but Joe would see a beef between Upper Arlington City Council and a nightclub's penchant for blasting "gangsta rap" as an opportunity to pen a uniquely Arlington rhyme?

Cruising down Tremont in my stepfather's Quattro,
Sipping on a 40-ounce caramel macchiato,

I suspect it would take a monumental force of will to stop reading after this opening line to a column from 2016:

> *The 8-foot woman stood talking to a juggler in a sombrero—just outside a room with a one-man band, Abraham Lincoln and a guy with a monkey on his shoulder.*

Later we learn that the monkey "furiously licked a red lollipop," an image made infinitely better because Joe, A.) took note of the candy's color, and B.) knew to share it with readers. Yet he never confuses brevity with levity. On the death of a pet, he writes, "I've always thought that a key part of the canine mystique is the adorable way they misinterpret our world."

In another column from this collection, he shares the story of a woman who, as a child, thought St. John Arena was named for her father, an ironworker who died in a fall there in 1955.

If there is a downside to Joe's writerly economy, it may be the sense that a column has ended too soon. But Joe is pro, and inevitably his columns end exactly where they should. To adapt a line from another column in this collection, they end when Joe has "said all that needed to be said."

A man of few words, Joe Blundo speaks volumes.

—Ted Decker, *Columbus Dispatch*

ACKNOWLEDGMENTS

I want to thank my parents for getting me a library card in New Castle, Pa., at age 6. I still remember my first checkout—a little blue children's book about an elephant. From then on, I read everything I could find. Reading leads to writing, and when people ask me how I became a writer, I often go back to that library card. At the *Columbus Dispatch,* I learned a lot from Luke Feck, an innovator, Hal Schellkopf, who loved words, and Mike Harden, the master column-writer. Mike Curtin was the editor who offered me the opportunity to try my hand at what Harden did. I took it, knowing I had at least three columns in me and uncertain what would happen beyond that. Twenty-one years later, the customers of the *Columbus Dispatch* continue to do me the honor of reading what I have to say. Sometimes they even agree with it. Finally, I couldn't have done the job without my family—both because they love me and because they accepted their roles as literary devices with great courage.

INTRODUCTION

I began writing my column, "So To Speak," in 1997. The opportunity came along after I'd spent 19 years at the *Columbus Dispatch* doing other things—reporting, headline-writing, layout, editing. Those things all required scrupulous objectivity. And then, all of a sudden, I could use the word "I" and say what I thought. It was like suddenly being granted the right to swim with a second arm.

As an avid reader of columns myself, I knew what annoyed me about them: predictability. So I set out to avoid that by not doing too much of any one thing.

The question I've heard most often from readers of my column is "How do you think of things to write about?"

In fact, I hear it so often that some years ago, I developed a speech about it. In it, I said that I have five rules of column writing:

1. A columnist must be irreverent about that which others are reverent. (In Columbus, that means not religion but the thing we hold more sacred—Buckeye football.)

2. You can write about your family as long as you don't do it too often. My method has been to wait for the big transitions—graduations, weddings, births, deaths. If I felt like I'd needed to do a sales job to convince readers that the event was column-worthy, I didn't write about it.

3. People with a passion make the best profiles. They also tend to have the least restrictive filters. They'll tell you anything and everything about the job, hobby, or cause that so animates them.

4. There's humor in trouble. When your car breaks down, it's a financial setback. When mine breaks down, it's a column. And I took every opportunity to participate in things I knew I'd do badly.

5. Columbus is inherently funny. Take advantage of it.

Looking over this collection of columns, I see that I need to add one more category: If you come to work with something you can't stop thinking about, you probably ought to write about it.

So, yes, occasionally I get serious because a columnist must sound human, and no human that I'd want to be acquainted with goes through life unaffected by the tragedies and outrages that make up so much of the news. But for the most part I try to be the relief from the news, rather than the amplifier of it.

This is my second book of collected columns, encompassing the years 2006 to 2017. There are still days when I come to work with a deadline in a few hours and no idea what I'm going to write about. It's like being carried toward a waterfall by a swift current. But then I consult my five-point list, remind myself that I can swim with both arms, and get to work.

HELLO, COLUMBUS

SEE STATEHOUSE WITH LESS CYNICISM: GO WITH CHILDREN

May 7, 2006

When disgust with Ohio politics is running high, take a Statehouse tour with kids.

All the wide-eyed innocence will renew your faith in representative government (although you might still be disgusted with Ohio politics).

Fourth- and fifth-graders from East Elementary School in Upper Sandusky were recently dazzled by the Statehouse.

"Sweet," one said.

"Awesome."

"Wicked" (the good kind).

Even the changes in elevation wowed them.

They hung over the railing in a Statehouse light court, looking down two floors and fighting the urge to spit. They stared longingly at wide marble banisters perfect for sliding.

Chris Matheney, the Statehouse education manager, had won them over early by showing up with a flintlock rifle. It was, of course, unloaded. (Some kid always asks.)

Before leading the group on a tour of the building, he gave them a rundown of his French and Indian War garb (waistcoat, breeches, leggings, wampum, Statehouse identification badge). You never know which detail will enthrall a kid.

"Wampum!" said Teal Shifflet, 10. "I never actually saw a wampum. Now I have."

Matheney quizzed the kids about Ohio and American history. Their answers were creative:

Q: What did American Indians wear to war?

A: Bikinis. (The correct answer is breechcloths, sort of like 18th-century bikinis.)

Q: Why did the Confederates fight the Civil War?

A: To get away from their wives. (The correct answer is—well, that probably was the correct answer for a few guys.)

School tours are cynicism-free.

When historian Mark Passerrello took fourth-graders from Edison Elementary in Ashland into the empty House chamber and explained that each representative has 115,000 bosses, no fourth-grader asked whether campaign contributors are bigger bosses than the rest of us.

They were mesmerized by the desks, the telephones, the electronic voting system and the golden eagle (one kid guessed that it's a vulture), which symbolizes the federal government.

School-age tourists include budding interior decorators (who want to comment on the pink walls) and legislators (who have bills they want to push).

Twin sisters Sarah and Hannah Chipps, 9, of Harrisburg, want to protect horses from slaughter and establish refuges for endangered species. Expect a letter, Rep. Dan Stewart.

The kids who disembark from buses at the Statehouse door might know only vaguely how the legislative process works, but there's nothing vague about their expectations: They want a fair world.

Passerrello took the Ashland students into the George Washington Williams Room, dedicated to the first black elected to the General Assembly. He explained that, in the 19th century, whites sometimes cheated blacks out of their right to vote.

There were gasps.

Who could vote unhindered in the 19th century? he asked.

The kids knew: white men.

"Who did that leave out?" he asked.

Madison Shilliday, 9, raised her hand and said, "Me."

Then the kids took their fourth-grade faith in liberty and justice for all, and got back on the buses.

It was a little sad to see them go.

THEIR CHILD IS A NUT BUT THEY'RE PROUD

Oct. 12, 2006

He was an irrepressible liberal from New York.

She was a conservative sorority girl from Mansfield.

Their differences drove them apart. But before the relationship ended, they conceived a mascot: Brutus Buckeye.

Official Brutus histories credit Ray Bourhis with creating the mascot in 1965, while he was a student at Ohio State University.

Bourhis, a San Francisco lawyer, is only too happy to acknowledge paternity. But he wants it known that there was also a mom: college girlfriend Sally (Huber) Lanyon.

Both parents are still a little miffed that OSU hasn't been more appreciative. For example, they weren't invited to their bigheaded boy's 40th birthday party last year.

"We really felt slighted," Lanyon said.

Bourhis jokes that the snub occurred because Brutus was born out of wedlock.

"They'd have to call him Brutus the *******."

Brutus' caretaker, OSU cheerleader coach Judy Bunting, said that no one meant to slight Lanyon and Bourhis. She just didn't know where they were.

In 1965, Bourhis and Lanyon collaborated to fill a void that seems shocking in retrospect.

In an already-mascot-rich world, OSU had no character risking heat exhaustion to cavort on the sidelines in an outlandish costume. (Bucky Badger had been perspiring for Wisconsin for 17 years by then.)

Bourhis, a member of the volunteer service organization Ohio Staters, proposed to fill the void with a deer.

"A buck—you know, with antlers."

But others insisted that the mascot had to be closer to a horse chestnut.

"So I said, 'How the hell are we going to dress a nut up and put it on the football field?'"

Lanyon and Bourhis have slightly different memories of the birth, but they agree that it involved papier-mâché and wire, and happened at Pi Beta Phi, her sorority.

"I had no artistic background," Lanyon said. "That's probably why it was so funny-looking at first."

Brutus, who looked something like an oversize army helmet with feet, was named by Kerry Reed, a student who submitted the winning entry in a name-the-mascot contest. (He's now a pastor at Gender Road Christian Church.)

Brutus made his debut at the Minnesota game. The identity of the first student to don the costume is lost in mascot history. But there's no doubt that the crowd loved the character—a big nut with changeable facial expressions.

"What I remember is that the place just went wild," Bourhis said.

He realized that a papier-mâché Brutus would never withstand the rigors of Big Ten football. So he found someone to make a lighter fiberglass costume to finish the season.

In the years since, Brutus has been through several metamorphoses, leading to today's more-agile version.

While Brutus endured, the Bourhis-Lanyon relationship didn't.

"I was this little conservative Protestant from Ohio, and he was this liberal Democrat from New York," Lanyon said. "I think that's why we didn't stay together."

Bourhis has established himself as a crusading lawyer known for taking on the insurance industry. He has appeared on *60 Minutes* and written a book, *Insult to Injury*.

Lanyon works as a consultant in Tucson, Ariz.

Both watch the Buckeyes on television, always hoping for a glimpse of their boy.

"I think they don't show him enough," the proud mom said.

GHOST TALES MORE KOOKY THAN SPOOKY

Oct. 19, 2008

What this city needs is a ghost judge.

Every October, "haunted tours" materialize all over town.

Can we really have that many buildings occupied by ghosts?

Check out the Web site of the Ohio Exploration Society sometime (www.ohioexploration.com). It collects tales that suggest everything from the Statehouse to a Pizza Hut in Hilliard is haunted.

Granted, the thought of spending eternity in a Pizza Hut is horrifying (although the garlic would protect ghosts from vampires). But if even Pizza Huts are haunted, then what isn't? The glut of questionable ghosts cheapens the paranormal experience.

I think we need to winnow the field. I will evaluate some local ghost stories and rule on whether they are true. Someone has to do it.

The story: The ghost of Abraham Lincoln dances with a woman at the Statehouse.

Ruling: not true

Reason: Abraham Lincoln was the president of the United States. He was commander in chief during the bloodiest struggle in our history. He was assassinated. Why would a guy who could haunt the White House or Gettysburg or Ford's Theatre pick the Ohio Statehouse instead?

No disrespect to the building, but come on: Claiming that Lincoln hangs out there is like claiming that Dracula abandoned his castle in favor of operating out of a branch dungeon in the suburbs.

If you had a choice between hovering over cabinet meetings at the White House or an Agriculture Committee hearing in the General Assembly, which would you choose?

The story: Camp Chase Confederate Cemetery is haunted.

Ruling: metaphorically true

Reason: Camp Chase holds the bodies of 2,260 Confederate prisoners of war who died far from home and family. The place is haunted all right—by history.

Against that reality, how lame is the ghost story of the "lady in gray" who supposedly wanders the cemetery searching for her lost love? Very lame.

She's probably based on a real person—Louisiana Briggs, a transplanted Southerner who used to leave flowers at the cemetery—but that's as close to convincing as the legend gets.

Ghostly ladies in various colors are paranormal clichés. Save them for less compelling locations. They can't compete with a cemetery full of tragically true stories.

The story: Various sites at Ohio State University are haunted.

Ruling: not true

Reason: Whether it's Mirror Lake or Orton Hall or miscellaneous fraternity houses, the haunted sites all contain some variation on the same themes: strange sounds, oddly dressed apparitions, inexplicable occurrences.

Well, on the grounds of a giant university full of frisky young adults, that's not paranormal, that's campus life.

An OSU building shrouded in calm—now that would be eerie. Find me one of those.

The story: A house in Walhalla Ravine is haunted.

Ruling: economically true

Reason: Tales of grisly murders and spooky occurrences, none of them the least bit convincing, hang over the ravine. Forget them. The stories are true in this sense only: The real-estate market is kind of scary right now. All houses are haunted.

THE FLAKES THAT DRIVE COLUMBUS INTO A FRENZY

Feb. 11, 2010

I love Columbus when it snows.

I'll bet that Cleveland, jaded by frequent blizzards, isn't as much fun. Another 2 feet of lake-effect snow? Ho-hum.

But in Columbus, snow is not just a weather condition. It's an occasion, a happening, an experience.

Here are the things I love about snow in Columbus:

The buzz

Rain is like the gloomy relative who shows up all too often and dampens the mood. But snow is a celebrity. People start talking about its arrival days in advance. It's a special guest that demands special preparations, so everyone hurries to stock up on provisions.

Does necessity explain the rush to the grocery store? Please. It's not as if we're going to be stranded in the mountains, like the Donner party. No one in Columbus lives more than five minutes from a Kroger.

The grocery rush is all part of Snow Anticipation Syndrome, that slightly giddy feeling we get when patches of white show up on Doppler radar in Indiana.

The clothes

In Columbus, snow is a come-as-you-are occasion. There is no dress code, but here are some fashion looks you might see:

- The "It's-Not-Snowing": A lot of Downtown power types favor this look, especially men. You will see them, briefcases in hand, hurrying along a sidewalk in suits that couldn't possibly be keeping them warm. Their mothers would be appalled.

- The Snow Bunny: This is the opposite of the "It's-Not-Snowing." Snow bunnies encase themselves in outerwear generously trimmed with white fur. Hawks have mistaken them for snowshoe hares.
- The Tow-Truck Driver: Just put on a pair of Carhartts and steel-toed shoes and command instant respect. People will assume that you have the power to free them from drifts.

The cancellations

Let's face it: Most of what's on our calendars, we'd rather not do anyway.

Work, school, meetings, doctor appointments, awkward social engagements: No one is too sorry to have them wiped off the schedule.

So, Columbus keeps the cancellation option on a hair trigger.

I say it's a smart policy. Of the things that can always excuse us from obligations—sickness, car breakdown, death and snow—snow is by far the most pleasant. Why not take advantage of it?

The drama

Snow causes us to become theatrical.

We don't have snowplow drivers; we have Snow Warriors. We don't have parking restrictions; we have Snow Emergencies. The schools don't take snow days; they take Calamity Days.

White flakes falling gently from the sky would not seem to merit such intense language.

On the other hand, when else will nature allow us to exercise our drama genes? Bears no longer roam the central Ohio countryside; floodwalls contain the rivers; crabgrass is under control.

So we've promoted snow to star in our nature tales. It fills a need—and fills our driveways—at the same time.

RAP ALERT: DON'T MESS WITH UA PLAYA

May 15, 2011

Upper Arlington will never be a hotbed of hip-hop now.

The City Council last week voted to stop a plan that would have stripped a troublesome nightclub (fights, drug activity, two shootings) of its liquor license. But, in return, the club had to agree to forsake "gangsta rap" in favor of a more mainstream playlist.

The agreement actually specified the pop playlist from WNCI (97.9 FM).

Under the deal as reported in The Dispatch, the Henderson Road club, once called Onyx, has been renamed Posh and agreed not to play music that portrays "violence and drug use of urban gang life."

Supposedly, the gangsta rap attracted actual gangstas. So that explains why they didn't switch to country. You'd have cowboys in pickup trucks all over the place.

Well, I hope that the whole thing works out for all concerned. But I do think a golden opportunity was missed. It occurs to me that affluent Arlington would be the perfect place to introduce a suburban style of gangsta rap.

I wrote a song to illustrate:

UA Playa by Joe-Z

I'm a UA playa, so don't get in my way
'Cause, down at the Chef-O-Nette, you know what they say:
When the playa comes around, all the posers be on guard
'Cause he's a bad *** ****** who will TP your yard.
Thanks to my parents paying for orthodontia,
All the ladies gather round and tell me, "Playa, we want ya.
"Our little hearts are thumpin', and our hormones are bubblin'
"'Cause you the finest gangsta between Grandview and Dublin."

Yeah, I'm a UA playa; don't be messin' with me.
I got a titanium lacrosse stick in my mom's SUV.
But I don't have to hit you, 'cause you know what I say?
The price tag alone will make you faint dead away.
Born in a split-level, Sam's Club food on the table,
Had a dial-up connection and only basic cable.
Mom lassoed a doctor in a lovesick condition.
Now I'll get into Harvard on a legacy admission.
Yeah, I'm a UA playa, and I got this whole place shook.
Stay out of my way, or I'll bully you on Facebook.
I'll turn my Yorkie loose and let him tear up your @#$
(Or at least not stop him when he lifts a leg on your grass).
At UAHS, I done hard time in detention
For toking on a Camel (unfiltered, need I mention?).
Came out of the Hole with my head high just the same,
And the posers all said, "Oh yeah, this playa's got game."
Cruising down Tremont in my stepfather's Quattro,
Sipping on a 40-ounce caramel macchiato,
30 mph in a 25 zone,
But the cops know I'm a playa, so they leave me alone.
Yeah, I'm a UA playa, and I guarantee
I'm a coldblooded killer (on the PlayStation 3).
I'm a UA playa; don't be tryin' to own me.
I'll do what I want (unless the council rezones me).

STATE FAIR ALWAYS MAKES A STRONG IMPRESSION

Aug. 4, 2011

Every big public event in central Ohio has a hidden theme.

Ohio State football games are all about devotion to ritual. Besides the score and the weather, very little changes from game to game: music, cheers, color scheme. Fans hate change. They like to brag about tailgating in the exact same spot for 35 years.

Red White & Boom is about bravery. You show your mettle by going Downtown with a half-million other people and finding a place to park.

The All American Quarter Horse Congress centers on sexiness. It's heavy with sequins, ostentatious belt buckles and equine studs.

And the Ohio State Fair?

Brawn. It's a brawn-a-thon.

Consider: The 2011 fair has featured Mama Lou, the strongwoman; the Omega Force Strongmen (Christian evangelists who lift heavy stuff); bench-pressing exhibitions; wrestling; boxing; roller derby; mixed martial arts; and bearlike men sawing logs.

I haven't even mentioned the giant squash, the giant iced tea, the giant Smokey Bear or the 500-pound chocolate pig.

Why this outpouring of muscularity?

Some would say state pride.

I say it's a natural reaction to being shown up by animals. Humans are the least-impressive species out there (unless you count politicians).

The cows are massive displays of bovine muscle and udders. The hogs are startlingly big. The horses are magnificent. Even the chickens, strutting around in their little cages, look as if they'd kick your butt if given half a chance.

People strolling the midway with a Belgian waffle and an excess of abdominal fat fare poorly in comparison. The best we can say for ourselves is that we're well-marbled.

So I figure we have to compensate by showing off human prowess and physicality where we can find it.

We bring in people to lift truck tires and tear phone books in half. (When the digital revolution finally kills the Yellow Pages, will we rip smartphones in half?) We book weightlifters. We invite people to punch each other.

The fair strikes me as brawnier than the Arnold Sports Festival, which outwardly appears to be all about brawn.

But, remember: Every event has a hidden theme.

The Arnold's is immortality.

The bodybuilders aspire to look like stone statues. They even pose in statuesque positions, as if they hope to be standing like that for centuries to come. Meanwhile, the crowd wanders amid booths full of energy drinks and dietary supplements promising near-supernatural benefits.

If my theory is correct, you will see the fair get even brawnier to compensate for people looking weaker and weaker next to the farm animals they so successfully breed.

By 2025, men will be pulling tractors, and the All-Ohio Ab and Bicep Corps. will march three times a day, twirling utility poles.

Being only human, I look forward to it.

MEAT GUYS: CAN WE AT LEAST GET A BUTT?

April 11, 2013

I searched in vain for an Ohio reference in the new meat names.

Nothing.

Boston got a roast. St. Louis got ribs. Santa Fe got a steak.

Would it have been too much to put, say, Cleveland's name on a chop or something?

I thought Ohio had political clout.

In case you haven't heard, the confusing nomenclature of meat cuts (beef top round cap steak boneless) is getting a makeover from the industry and the government.

The new names will be equally confusing (Santa Fe steak—does that really help?) but mostly shorter.

The renaming project spells the demise of the pork butt, which was actually shoulder meat and will now be, for some reason, Boston roast.

You see the injustice? Ohio has Cincinnati, a city once so full of hogs that its nickname was Porkopolis, yet Boston gets the pork butt? Unfair: Boston already has the cream pie and the baked bean. It doesn't need a roast, a butt or whatever you want to call it.

And it's not as if there aren't enough meat names to go around.

I counted about 120 cuts of beef alone. Ohioans wouldn't have demanded a tenderloin or a rib-eye. We're humble. We would have been just fine with a Toledo under-blade pot roast or a Dilles Bottom top round.

I'd also lobby for Lake Erie wine steak instead of merlot steak, the name chosen for the cut formerly known as beef bottom round boneless.

The beef people have long seemed a little light in the language department to me. Only in their world do cows have arms but not legs. You'll find a chuck arm roast and a chuck arm steak but not a single leg of anything on either the old or new list of meat names.

They've also added flank steak fingers. That's actually disturbing.

Even where you think they're being precise, they're not: The seven-bone chuck steak comes in a boneless variety.

Things that sounded too much like cow parts (beef loin flap meat) have been given more-pretentious names (sirloin bavette).

The pork names aren't much better, although they do acknowledge that hogs have legs.

Still, the renaming makes some pork sound like beef: It has a rib-eye and a T-bone on a pig. And—get this—there's no pork chop. The generic name has given way to more specific descriptions, such as tenderloin chop.

Most dismaying is that a certain Midwestern state capital gets its name on a pork roast and a pork steak.

Columbus? Indianapolis?

Nope, little Des Moines, Iowa.

Granted, it's a pork power, but couldn't it have given either the roast or the steak to Columbus?

Our body-mass index is pretty strong evidence that we are doing our part to keep pork consumption high.

One cut of beef or pork is all I ask.

Look, there's already a chuck eye roast. Let's add some poetry and call it the Buckeye chuck eye.

It would still be in good taste.

RAIL-SPLITTING PERSONALITIES TURN HEADS IN CAPITAL CITY

April 13, 2013

An assemblage of Abes invaded the Statehouse yesterday to stand where President Lincoln stood, speak where he spoke and—in one case—lie where he lay.

The Association of Lincoln Presenters—impersonators of the Great Emancipator—toured Ohio's seat of government as part of its national convention.

The event has brought to town about 40 Abes, 15 Marys (the president's wife) and one Robert (the Lincolns' son, portrayed by Jesse Noily, a 13-year-old history enthusiast from Oakland, Calif.).

"These are really nice people," said Randy Duncan, a Lincoln presenter from Carlinville, Ill. "I don't know if we start out that way or if enough Lincoln rubs off that we become nicer."

Duncan, 51, has a story similar to those of other presenters: People thought his beard and lanky 6-foot-1-inch frame gave him a resemblance to the 6-foot-4 Lincoln. He took it from there.

He was standing in the convention headquarters, the Ramada Columbus East Airport hotel, wearing a pocket watch (19th-century model), uncreased pants (pants weren't creased in Lincoln's day), high black boots ($200 and handmade) and the requisite stovepipe hat.

"The more of the little things you get right, the more they add up," said Duncan, a plant manager.

At the Statehouse, the Lincolns took turns being photographed next to a plaque marking the presumed spot where the future president spoke on a visit in 1859.

They also occupied the House of Representatives, where presenter Jerry Payn of Wooster re-enacted a speech that the newly elected Lincoln gave there in 1861.

And they milled around the rotunda, where Lincoln's body lay in state in 1865.

Presenter Rick Miller, a yoga teacher from the Pittsburgh area, couldn't resist stretching out on the rotunda floor himself for a photo.

"I want to show this pose to my yoga students," he said.

The group next headed to the home of Gen. William Tecumseh Sherman in Lancaster, then to Reynoldsburg for an Encore Academy performance of *My American Cousin,* the play Lincoln was watching when he was shot.

"This time we're staying to the end," more than one presenter quipped.

Similarities to Lincoln are a favorite topic.

Stan Wernz, 77, of Cincinnati noted that he was born on Lincoln Avenue.

Jim "the Great Pretender" Sayre, 77, of Lawrenceburg, Ky., said that, like Lincoln, he was born poor in Kentucky, was educated in a one-room schoolhouse and wed a woman named Mary.

"But his wife was quite wealthy—and that's where the similarities end."

Robert Brugler, a convention organizer and retired schoolteacher who lives in Worthington, said Lincoln's resurgence in pop culture through movies such as *Lincoln* and *Abraham Lincoln: Vampire Hunter* has inspired a host of new questions.

For the record, he liked Lincoln and thinks that hunting vampires would have been out of character.

"Lincoln told people he couldn't even cut the head off a chicken," said Brugler, 62. "He did not like blood."

Most of the presenters have acts they perform for civic groups, schools and historical societies. A few have been in movies or on TV shows.

And they've grown accustomed to attracting attention.

John Mansfield, a 6-foot-6 presenter from Nashville, Tenn., said he has signed autographs and been thanked for freeing the slaves and occasionally berated for having Union loyalties.

"There are some very staunch Rebels out there who are still fighting the war."

HIGH HOPES AMONG FANS PUT OSU ON FIRE WATCH

Aug. 29, 2013

Several Buckeyes football fans have spontaneously burst into flames this week, Columbus officials revealed yesterday.

Sky-high expectations for the new Ohio State season are setting off an emotional chain reaction that's causing the spontaneous fan combustion, the officials said.

High-proof liquor heightens the risk.

"All that emotion and energy have to go somewhere," said Pete Sakes, a fan-behavior specialist for the Columbus Division of Sports Phenomena.

"Guys get themselves all worked up about Urban Meyer's spread offense, internal body temperatures rise, somebody pours a scotch, and the next thing you know—poof!"

In the most recent incident, a man at a North Side sports bar became overly agitated as he extolled the virtues of quarterback Braxton Miller. Suddenly, his hair began smoking and flames leapt from his head.

"Fortunately," Sakes said, "the people at the next table were able to extinguish him with a pitcher of beer."

In another case, an overwrought caller to a radio talk show ignited at home during an extended rant about why OSU will go undefeated.

"His wife used a broom to beat out the flames—with a lot of enthusiasm, from what I hear," Sakes reported.

Officials are still trying to get details on a third case, which apparently happened at a West Side sports bar that today bears a sign warning Buckeyes fans that bursting into flames violates the state's no-smoking law.

The incidents seem to confirm a threat that OSU has long feared: In the 1990s, OSU commissioned Battelle to study whether overly passionate tailgaters could spontaneously combust, sparking grass fires that, during a dry September, might spread to campus buildings.

The research institute concluded that such a phenomenon was possible but unlikely because expectations, even among Buckeyes fans, probably couldn't reach levels necessary to spark ignition.

But the 12–0 season in 2012 and a weak 2013 schedule might well have boosted expectations to that critical point.

"It's a real safety concern for game day," Sakes said. "The intensity of emotion will be even greater than it is now, and we also have the presence of volatile gases caused by baked-bean consumption. We could have people going up like tiki torches."

OSU reportedly plans to dispatch teams of "fan calmers" to tailgate parties for Saturday's opener against Buffalo.

Their mission will be to explain the odds against another undefeated season, mist fans who work themselves into a tizzy and watch for people whose heads are beginning to smoke.

CREATURES OF THE NIGHT REALIZE WORST FEAR

Oct. 29, 2013

Ghosts, zombies, vampires and other supernatural creatures are leaving the Columbus area because, they say, it's too hard to scare people here.

For one thing, the frustrated ghouls say, it's tough to compete with the well-established fears that already preoccupy central Ohioans.

"Oh, sure, they'll let out a shriek or two if you jump out of the shadows," said a vampire, who asked to remain anonymous because his employer might object to his sneaking out at night to drink the blood of maidens.

"But if you really want to terrify them, tell them it's going to snow or that the Buckeyes will remain stuck at fourth place in the BCS rankings."

Compounding the problem is the central Ohio tendency toward Midwestern pragmatism, as evidenced by the experience of a werewolf who has found his nighttime forays less than intimidating.

"Every time there's a full moon, I go out and howl and snarl and whatnot," he said. "And, sure enough, a pet-rescue group shows up, and—next thing you know—I'm being adopted by a family of four in Westerville.

"I've come pretty close to being neutered at least twice that way. Talk about scary."

Ghosts have also found the area less than receptive, particularly in the more affluent suburbs—where people have a big stake in property values.

"When people with a $300,000 mortgage hear noises in the wall, they don't think ghost," a ghost said. "They think termites.

"You go to all that trouble to send people a message from beyond the grave, and all you get for it is a face full of insecticide."

The ghost, known as the Lady in Blue, tried going door to door to scare people but still had no success.

"You knock on doors in the suburbs, and people automatically assume you're collecting for a high-school sports team. One night, I scared absolutely no one but raised $34 for new lacrosse jerseys."

The struggles of super-natural creatures become more acute as Halloween approaches, a zombie said.

"People think I'm a front-yard decoration," he lamented. "It's dehumanizing."

Discouraged by their reception here, many zombies have left the area and a few others have changed careers.

Some play dead soldiers in Civil War re-enactments; others have become crash-test dummies.

At least two have been elected to the state legislature.

"It's a sad state of affairs," the anonymous vampire said. "But if I can't get the terror I deserve here, I'll move.

"Most of us became supernatural because we love the adrenaline rush. I'm not about to give up on that. You have to follow your nightmares, as I like to say."

GREATEST APE OF OUR ZOO JUST AS HE IMAGINED

Dec. 23, 2014

After years of trying, So To Speak finally scored a dream interview with Colo the gorilla.

In other words: I might have just dreamed it.

Colo, the first gorilla born in captivity, celebrated her 58th birthday yesterday at the Columbus Zoo and Aquarium, where she arrived to great hoopla in 1956.

Here are highlights from our fantastic question-and-answer session:

Q: Colo, you have been in captivity your entire life. Have you ever wanted to try living in the jungle?

A: I've thought it might be fun—if I had the right equipment and if I knew it was just for a weekend.

Otherwise, I'd probably be sitting in the dirt crying—like Reese Witherspoon in *Wild*. I've been a city dweller all my life.

Q: Jack Hanna has been a regular guest on *Late Show With David Letterman* for years. Why didn't you ever appear on the show with him?

A: We talked about it, but the timing just never worked. Plus, you know Dave: He wanted me to climb to the top of the Empire State Building while carrying Justin Bieber.

I said: "Honey, I'll leave that King Kong stuff to younger gorillas. This girl takes elevators."

Q: I've heard that you were jealous about the fuss over the giraffes in the new "Heart of Africa" exhibit.

A: Not jealous—I love giraffes. They're doing a great job, ambling around and eating out of peoples' hands. But . . .

Q: But?

A: Well, let's be honest: They can't compete with primates in the personality department.

When the zoo bigwigs were planning the exhibit, I told them: "Guys, what you want is impressive height and effervescence. Ditch the giraffes and put a half-dozen bonobos on stilts. People will never get bored."

Q: So you see yourself as a performer?

A: Yes, and I try to give some subtlety to the role. You have to know the audience.

People want to laugh at otters and tremble at snakes. But they want to connect with gorillas.

You know that thing where I turn my back to spectators as if I'm ignoring them? That makes them long for me even more.

Q: So you manipulate human beings?

A: You say that as if you think it's a difficult thing to do. Have you never watched a jewelry commercial? It's not rocket science.

Q: Finally, I've always wanted to ask a non-human primate: Do you believe in evolution?

A: My goodness, no.

Me? Related to those tourists who tap on the glass and make monkey noises while I'm trying to eat? Unthinkable.

OHIO STATE OBSESSION TOO MUCH FOR THIS ANA

Feb. 10, 2015

A certain movie has inspired me to write a script of my own. Call it *Fifty Shades of Scarlet and Gray*:

Sparks fly when Ana, a beautiful but innocent college student, meets Christian, a 27-year-old billionaire and obsessive Ohio State fan.

Christian, a control freak, won't allow the relationship to get physical, though, unless Ana signs a contract agreeing to certain conditions.

Confused, Ana seeks the advice of her worldly friend Kate.

"What kind of conditions?" Kate asks.

"For foreplay, I have to simulate an Ohio Stadium pregame show—with marching band and public-address announcer and everything. Is that, like, normal?"

"Only for an OSU fan," Kate says. "Do you need help finding sousaphone players?"

Ana is athletic and sports-minded, but she finds Christian's football fixation difficult to fathom: He wants her to whisper the entire 1968 OSU roster in his ear; he demands that she tape her ankles; he wants her to enter his shower, which sprays Gatorade instead of water.

Finally, he confesses that he had a troubled childhood: The John Cooper-era failures against Michigan, the '98 Michigan State upset and the long championship drought all convinced him that he hadn't rooted hard enough for his team.

He vowed then to incorporate OSU football into every aspect of his life.

When she tries to soothe him by stroking his hair, Ana is flagged for illegal use of hands. (Christian likes to take a Big Ten officiating crew on dates.)

Ana again seeks Kate's counsel.

"I think he's into domination," Ana says.

"Why?"

"He asked me to sell unlicensed apparel on a street corner because he thought it would be sexy to slap me with a lawsuit."

"Wow, that is kinky."

Christian continues to woo Ana: He plants her a grove of buckeye trees. He gives her a puppy named Urban. When she pleases him, he pastes Buckeye leaves on her head.

But the night he asks her to scrimmage in the bedroom proves to be the breaking point.

"He insisted we both wear full pads," a disgusted Ana later tells Kate. "And then he ordered me to get into a three-point stance so he could bull-rush me, like Joey Bosa putting pressure on Oregon."

"Did you use your safe word to stop him?" Kate asks.

"No, I pancaked the little creep into the carpet. He might be rich and obsessed with the Buckeyes, but he doesn't know a thing about playing football."

"That pretty much describes everyone in a luxury box at Ohio Stadium, honey. Just sayin'."

A FAIR HISTORY THAT'S DEEP-FRIED IN ABSURDITY

July 30, 2015

On the heels of the opening of the 162nd Ohio State Fair, here's an almost-factual history of the annual event:

1849: In a freak accident, a wagon bearing cornmeal and a wagon bearing sausages collide and spill their cargo at a spot where a roadside food vendor is heating a vat of oil. The mishap results in the first corn dog.

Curious farmers converge on the scene and are soon arguing about whose cows are prettier. Just then, a troupe of jugglers and clowns happens by in a stagecoach.

By the next Sunday, preachers are declaring that such an unlikely convergence of events must be a sign that God wants Ohio to have a yearly event in which farmers eat fat-laden food and show off their livestock while jugglers and clowns annoy them.

1850: The state legislature creates the Ohio State Fair. To protect agricultural productivity, it declares that the fair cannot begin until it's too hot to do anything else. (To this day, by law, the fair cannot start until heat and humidity reach life-threatening levels.)

1879: Ohio native Thomas Edison announces that he will make the world's first flight in a heavier-than-air craft at the fair. But, after consuming four funnel cakes, two elephant ears and a blooming onion, he can't get the plane off the ground.

Embarrassed, Edison gives up on airplanes and invents the lightbulb instead. When Orville and Wilbur Wright of Ohio make the first successful flight 24 years later, they carry several Belgian waffles in a subtle dig at Edison.

1909: James A. Rhodes is born in a stable at the fairgrounds. He lives there all his life, even while serving 17 terms as governor.

1951: Fair officials announce a major building campaign because they have run out of structures to name after politicians.

1978: In an attempt to promote better nutrition, the fair board switches to a margarine cow. Protests ensue, and the margarine cow is ultimately taken off display and used to grease the Giant Slide.

1989: The fair restricts the Sale of Champions to livestock, ending the practice of large corporations bidding on state legislators.

"There is already an established market for that," a fair official says.

1997: A nationwide blue-ribbon shortage forces the fair to close early.

2013: A consultant recommends that the fair become hipper by merging with ComFest.

Merger talks quickly fall apart when the fair balks at using Smokey Bear to promote the legalization of marijuana.

An official explains: "We have 10,000 smells, rides that turn people upside down, flashing lights, pig races. The fair is already a mind-altering experience."

AFTER 'OVAL,' OSU HAS PLENTY MORE TO TRADEMARK

March 12, 2017

The compulsive trademarkers at Ohio State University are at it again.

They want to trademark "the Oval."

I mean the name and the image of the campus green space to which it refers, not the shape.

So you'll still be able to sell a hard-boiled egg without getting a cease-and-desist letter from university lawyers.

(But if the university's scientists figure out how to breed chickens that lay scarlet and gray eggs, then I'm not so sure. OSU has a trademark on the color scheme.)

Other trademarked items at OSU: Urban Meyer, Brutus Buckeye, The 'Shoe, Woody Hayes, the buckeye leaf and—my favorite—the gestures that spell out O-H-I-O. You can barely extend an arm at OSU without hitting a trademark.

How much further can this trademarking trend go? Much further.

Here are some news stories from the near future:

OSU trademarks a smell

The mingled scents of bratwurst, beer, pheromones and heavy-equipment exhaust have been trademarked by Ohio State University.

"These aromas powerfully evoke the ambience of game day on a campus constantly under construction," a university lawyer said. "As such, they are part of our brand. If you want to smell like us, please contact the Office of Trademark & Licensing."

OSU trademarks student

Sophomore Emily X. Emplary has been trademarked by Ohio State University.

"I guess it's kind of an honor," said Emplary, 19, of Bucyrus. "They used an algorithm to identify a student whose age, background, achievements and activities typified the Ohio State experience. I fit so perfectly, they decided I was, like, a symbol of the university."

Emplary said she's still allowed to use her name, provided that she adds the words "a registered trademark of The Ohio State University."

"It makes meeting people a little awkward," she noted.

OSU trademarks fan behavior

Ohio State University has trademarked extreme football-fan behaviors that it says are unique to the school.

"Many schools have devoted fans, but only at Ohio State do they set themselves on fire to celebrate a victory, pluck out their own eyeballs in fits of anxiety or postpone childbirth until after the Michigan game," a university spokesman said. "So it's prudent to trademark them."

OSU trademarks 'trademark'

Ohio State University has trademarked the word trademark because it is so closely associated with the school.

"We are famous for our trademarking," a university spokesman said. "So trademarking trademark was necessary to protect our brand identity.

"Of course, if Notre Dame or Harvard want to trademark something, they're still free to do so. They'll just have to pay us to use the word trademark. It makes sense, don't you think?"

THE LAST JEDI, WITH A TOUCH OF BUCKEYE

Dec. 14, 2017

In the entertainment scoop of the year, So To Speak has obtained the screenplay for *Star Wars: The Last Jedi.*

You can amaze and confuse your friends by reciting lines of dialogue from it before it even opens.

Here's the "plot":

Rey, a resistance fighter battling the sinister First Order in an intergalactic struggle, finally locates the long-sought Jedi knight Luke Skywalker.

He has been hiding for decades in the obscure Midwestern metropolis of Columbus, Ohio, where he serves as a justice of the Ohio Supreme Court under the assumed name O'Skywalker.

"I just blended in with other justices—O'Neill, O'Donnell, O'Connor," Luke explains to Rey. "And even though I wear a hoodie and carry a lightsaber, most people think O'Neill is the odd one."

"You're telling me," Rey said. "I said hello to him on the street just now, and he promptly added me to his list of 50-some lovers."

Luke agrees to teach Rey some lightsaber tricks on the lawn of the Columbus Commons, but no sooner have they started than four First Order storm troopers rush to arrest them.

The rebels flee north on High Street, then hide in a strange photo booth at the Greater Columbus Convention Center. Unfortunately, it's a digital art installation that displays their faces on a 14-foot-tall head. Within seconds, they are captured.

"Luke, you've got to summon the Force," Rey pleads.

"I can do better than that," he replies.

Luke promises the dimwitted storm troopers that he will go peacefully if they will just contort their limbs into the shape of a consonant and three vowels as a sign of goodwill.

When they do, they are instantly vaporized for illicit use of the O-H-I-O gestures.

"Was it the Force?" an astonished Rey asks as they run away.

"No, it was the OSU trademark police," Luke replies. "They're more powerful than the Force. They even zapped Yoda for singing the first line of 'Carmen Ohio' as 'Oh, come, sing Ohio's praise, let us.'"

Luke and Rey need to leave Columbus now that the First Order knows their whereabouts. She suggests walking to Canada by following the Rover pipeline.

"No one would dare follow us through that swamp of foul substances," she says.

But Luke has a better idea. He leads her to a backroom at Mapfre Stadium. Inside, they find dozens of crates hidden under tarps.

"We can hide in one of these," he says. "They're being sneaked to Austin, Texas, a few at a time."

Rey reads the name on the crate's return address: "Precourt. Sounds familiar. What's his first name?"

"In this town," says Luke as he climbs in, "we call him Darth."

FAMILY MATTERS

FAMILY LIFE GIVES HIM RIGHT STUFF FOR HIGH COURT

July 17, 2005

After careful reflection, I've decided I will accept President Bush's nomination to serve on the U.S. Supreme Court.

If he calls. I'm sure it will be because I have broad experience in settling domestic disputes.

I know what my nomination will mean: tough confirmation hearings in which my lack of legal training will be raised again and again by partisan opponents. To them, I say: Does the education I gained from watching countless hours of *Law & Order* count for nothing?

I think my judicial record speaks for itself. Allow me to briefly review my most important legal opinions:

Blundo vs. Blundo

In the landmark 1996 case, I ruled that my children would have separate-but-equal accommodations in the back seat of a Toyota for the duration of a 12-hour drive to Myrtle Beach, S.C.

The case turned on what remedies could be applied when the petitioner thought that equality had been compromised.

To quote from my opinion:

"An accidental and inconsequential intrusion by Child A onto Child B's 'side' of the back seat does not constitute a material breach of the agreement between the two parties. But Child A is hereby notified that throwing Cheetos at Child B constitutes neither accidental nor inconsequential intrusion. I'm not going to say this again.

"Moreover, Child B's threat to respond to Child A's aggression by making herself carsick and throwing up on him is expressly prohibited. Do you hear me, young lady?

"Both parties are instructed to maintain silence until we hit the South Carolina border. Failure to do so will result in one or both being encased in bubble wrap and duct tape for the next 100 miles."

Blundo vs. Blundo

In the 1998 case, Child A petitioned the court for relief from the obligation to remove seven months' worth of dirty laundry, 11 partially eaten bags of potato chips and four dozen empty beverage cans from "his" bedroom.

My opinion put the constitutional right to privacy in the proper perspective:

"Just as a citizen's freedom of speech does not permit him to yell 'Fire!' in a crowded theater, Child A's right to privacy does not grant him authority to maintain a compost pile in his room. Now get this mess cleaned up before I call the Environmental Protection Agency."

Blundo vs. Blundo
vs. Blundo vs. Blundo

The dispute from 2004 involved four parties with different tastes in pizza. To summarize: Party A likes anchovies, while Parties B, C and D consider the mere sight of them cruel and unusual punishment. Moreover, they disagree among themselves on the best pizza.

The case posed a severe test of my judicial temperament because I was involved in the dispute on the pro-anchovy side.

My ruling set a new dietary precedent: "Party A's eminently reasonable suggestion that the pizza be ordered with anchovies on one-fourth of it has been rejected by Parties B, C and D on grounds that the proximity to anchovies is as bad as the eating of them.

"Party A finds this line of reasoning to be without merit. He could make the same claim against pepperoni, which oozes grease like a ruptured supertanker. But in the interests of preserving domestic tranquility, he agrees to waive his rights to anchovies.

"Nothing in this ruling shall be construed as permission to order a pizza with pineapple. Now, for heaven's sake, let's eat."

AREA DAD SURVIVES ANONYMOUS DAUGHTER'S FIRST DANCE

Oct. 25, 2005

It's a good thing I'm not writing this column about my 15-year-old daughter's homecoming dance, because she would kill me.

Instead, I'm writing in general about 15-year-olds who are preparing for their first formal dance. Any resemblance to persons living or dead or appearing as a dependent on my tax return is purely coincidental.

Let's say a 15-year-old who is definitely not my daughter came home and announced that she was going to the homecoming dance. In a dress. With a boy. How would I react?

I would lose consciousness. Wasn't it just yesterday that her idea of formalwear was black flip-flops? What happened?

Well, young teens can be a little like caterpillars. They go into cocoons before bursting forth as butterflies.

In their cocoon phase, at about 13 or 14, they retreat behind a wall of intense friendships and electronic communication devices. Physically, they are present (you can tell by the grocery bill). But mentally and socially, they are elsewhere.

To speak to a teen who is simultaneously playing a computer game, instant-messaging friends and listening to an iPod, you have to break through three levels of technology and interrupt secretive conversations. You have a better chance of barging into a meeting of the National Security Council.

The standoffishness is partly a survival tactic: The middle-school code of honor says that 13-year-olds, when faced with a choice of parental interaction or death, must choose death.

At about 15, kids begin to re-emerge, and you realize what they must have been instant-messaging about all that time: the homecoming dance.

Not only is she going, but she already has the dress, the shoes and the purse picked out. This from a child who once would have debated whether dinner with the queen of England was reason enough to change into her nice jeans.

What should you do when confronted with such an abrupt transition? Very little.

Fifteen-year-olds don't want parental fusses made. Pretend not to notice. Keep your responses to one syllable: "Wow. Cool. Good."

In truth, parents really have very little to do other than heed their usual role of supplying money.

In fact, if a 15-year-old's mother should decide to knit, say, a furry blue shawl that would be just perfect with the homecoming dress, she should restrain herself. She runs the risk of the 15-year-old (who is absolutely not my daughter) refusing to wear it on the grounds that it will "look like I killed Cookie Monster."

This brings us to the matter of boys.

As soon as a 15-year-old girl who is not my daughter announces that she's going to a homecoming dance, all 15-year-old boys begin to look 8 feet tall.

You think illogical thoughts such as: No daughter of mine is going out with a boy who shaves!

But don't worry too early. The pairing arrangements for a homecoming dance are extremely fluid. It's better to stand on the sidelines and wait for reports from the field on who is going with whom. It tends to change by the hour.

Also, dates at 15 often resemble the great caribou migration: The kids go out in huge herds that stop frequently to graze.

If all goes well, a 15-year-old who is positively not my daughter will go to the dance in a brown-and-turquoise dress with a polite young man in a dark suit.

She will have a good time, and her dad will have survived another transition.

Or so I hear.

FATHER'S DAY: A PROCLAMATION

June 21, 2007

Because this is a day of particular importance, I've decided to issue a proclamation:

Whereas today is Father's Day;

And whereas your father played a pivotal role in bringing you into the world;

And whereas he subsequently taught you to ride a bike, spit, recognize the spread offense and respect the five-second rule for eating food dropped on the floor;

And whereas you went to your mother for nurturing but to your father when you wanted to display your newfound ability to belch *The William Tell Overture* or turn your eyelids inside out;

And whereas your father carefully schooled you in safety procedures when handling fireworks (to wit: "Don't tell your mother");

And whereas your sense of adventure was honed by your father's self-reliant approach to finding unfamiliar addresses without asking directions (because if your dad can't find his way there, it probably doesn't exist);

And whereas you have recognized your father's contributions in the past by bestowing on him tokens such as cuff links, barbecue mitts and coffee mugs, not that he's complaining;

Now therefore be it resolved that:

1. All sons and daughters shall apply desirable adjectives to their fathers today, particularly "rugged."

   To wit:

   a. "Dad, would you get the lid off this pickle jar by twisting it with your viselike hands or charming it with your rugged good looks, or both?"

b. "Dad, you snore, but it's the rugged snore of a man accustomed to taking life head-on."

2. No person shall make a father feel irrelevant today by bringing up the scientific discovery of a hammerhead shark who seems to have impregnated herself without male participation. (Right, like we're supposed to believe she wasn't seeing a grouper on the side.)
3. All persons tempted to give their dads underwear, after-shave or a necktie for Father's Day shall not fail to first consider a tool driven by a powerful motor.
4. If it's cordless, all the better.
5. No person shall use Father's Day as an occasion to discuss the male brain.

   It is inevitably portrayed in scientific studies as largely consisting of primitive reptilian impulses overlaid with an evolved capacity for remembering sports statistics.

   (As if all dads do in their leisure time is sun themselves on rocks and compare batting averages in the American League Central.)
6. No person shall, on Father's Day, make exaggerated accusations concerning the fatherly habit of leaving hairs in the sink, socks on the floor or empty rolls on the toilet-paper holder.

   Such occurrences are rare and usually the result of dads concentrating on more important matters—including, but not limited to, batting averages in the American League Central.
7. No person shall, on Father's Day, tune into a situation comedy in which the dad is portrayed as a lazy bumbler whose deepest thoughts are about golf, sex and beer.

   In other words, all situation comedies.
8. All persons shall, upon seeing their dads today, make appropriate gestures of affection and offer large quantities of food.

But, please, no hammerhead shark.

WHEN SON BECOMES A MAN, DAD STILL FRETS

June 13, 2006

My son, Noah, graduated from Ohio University last week and is now undeniably an adult.

Our health-insurance company helped us celebrate by dropping him from my policy the day he was handed his diploma.

Of course, parenthood comes with no such cutoff date, so we're launching him into the world with stopgap major-medical coverage and secondhand dishes.

Among the landmark events of having a child reach adulthood is that it reverses the flow of stuff.

For 22 years, he was a net contributor to the stuff stream in our house. Now he becomes a relief conduit into which we can direct old furniture, unused tools and surplus utensils.

There are other advantages.

I found his college graduation a far more satisfying transition than his high-school graduation.

When Noah graduated from high school, I knew we were on the verge of a major test of our parenting.

After 18 or so years as on-site supervisors, we would suddenly become something like the home office: 90 miles away and forced to rely on reports from the field for assurance that company policy was being observed.

It's tough on a middle-aged parent. You still have enough long-term memory left to recall your own college experiences, many of which you fervently hope that your child will not repeat. But if he does, you hope he won't tell you about it.

Of course, college administrators know this. That's why they set up orientations in such a way that parents and offspring are separated as much as possible.

Otherwise—in a reverse of the first day of preschool—Mom and Dad would be clinging to the child's leg, wailing with separation anxiety.

Well, who can blame these poor parents? After 18 years of being indispensable, you don't just become a casual observer overnight.

I figure that's why God designed 18-year-olds to think they're indestructible. Otherwise, they'd never be able to overcome their parents' resistance to letting them out of the house.

Four years later, there he stood, with a degree in journalism. He deserves 99 percent of the credit, but I like to think our worrying helped a little.

Now, about that career choice: Yes, I suppose I influenced him, perhaps by writing fun stuff for too long. He has never lived with someone who had to cover horrors such as double homicides or the state legislature.

With degree in hand, Noah is off to Youngstown to do a newspaper internship. Having grown up near there, I can tell you that the city's image is only half-accurate—a shame if you're an aspiring journalist.

As for me, I'm undergoing a worry shift.

I worry less about this young adult now than about the country where he'll try to make a living. I don't want it to become so cruel, cynical and chaotic that a good guy can't get a break.

By coincidence, Noah's commencement came a day after I addressed the graduating class of Columbus State Community College.

I told the graduates they should have money deducted from their paychecks every week and put in a place out of reach of plastic cards.

The strong message I'm getting from Washington's unwillingness to deal with the Social Security crisis, the Medicare crisis, the health-care crisis, the pension crisis, the energy crisis and the national-debt crisis is this: You're on your own, pal.

I know that during Noah's career the news will always be interesting.

I hope that sometimes it's even good.

MOM'S SONG RESONATED IN KEY OF LIFE

Dec. 3, 2006

We put a ukulele in my mother's casket.

No one who knew her had to ask why. She was known for her love of music.

Her fondest wish for me was that I would become a musician, but I didn't have her passion. So, to mark her death, I can't write a concerto. But I can write a column for her.

My mom, born Catherine DiGiacomo, was the daughter of Italian immigrants. She lived her entire 82 years in New Castle, Pa. I never heard her express a desire to live anywhere else: Leaving behind her parents and her sisters would have been unthinkable.

She must have been born with musical inclinations. On the street where her family lived, she was known as the little girl who pounded incessantly on a patient neighbor's piano.

No doubt she grew up imagining herself singing with one of the big bands she loved, but her real-world goals were more modest: She wanted to be a mother.

It almost didn't happen.

In 1948, my mom married Ben Blundo, a tall, handsome World War II veteran who lived on the same street she did. They lost two newborn daughters to illness during their first years of marriage.

I grew up hearing about those lost sisters, but kids have no context for understanding such events. Only after I had children of my own did I realize what it must have taken for her to try yet again.

I was the result.

My favorite picture of the two of us shows me as a toddler sitting on her lap. She's young and pretty, and we look contented, as only mother and child can look. By then, she must have convinced herself that I wasn't going to die, like her other babies.

She had my brother, Ben, two years later, and my sister, Judy, three years after that.

My mom had several pronounced anxieties. She loathed swimming and airplanes, avoided dogs and thought herself incapable of learning to drive.

Consequently, she and my dad went everywhere together. People thought of them as a unit: Catherine and Ben. She called him "baby doll" and "dearie."

After we grew up, they found a hobby together: She sang in the Sweet Adelines barbershop chorus, and he went to all the shows and social events with her.

Losing my dad suddenly to a heart attack in 1981 was the greatest tragedy of my mom's life. But we knew she would survive it when she decided to learn how to drive. She wasn't good at it—she never overcame a reluctance to make left turns—but she did it.

Music was another thing that pulled her through. She sang in choruses and the church choir and to her grandchildren, grandnieces and grandnephews. My mother never went to bars, but she kept a karaoke machine in her kitchen.

Alzheimer's disease began closing in on her when she reached her late 70s.

She slowly receded from us. It felt as if I were standing at the familiar back door of her house, watching her but unable to close the distance. Once in a while, she'd look up and wave, maybe say hello. But I couldn't get in, and she couldn't get out.

We lost her the day after Thanksgiving, with several generations of her extended family at her bedside.

The ukulele in her casket was something she bought herself when she was young and single. She'd take it to parties because she thought every good time called for a little singing.

It's a sweet little music-maker, not flashy or loud but more than capable of adding some harmony to the world.

Just like Mom.

POODLE PUTS STAMP OF APPROVAL ON PARK

June 21, 2007

So, I took Mickey, my blind poodle, to Alum Creek Dog Park.

It was a major event in her life because this dog rarely goes anywhere. When she gets in the car, it usually means one thing: vet's office.

She loves the vet's office. We board her there when we leave town, and I'm guessing she thinks it's a spa.

"Yes, I'm going to the vet's office," I imagine her saying while stretching luxuriously. "It'll be so good to get away."

By contrast, the dog park on Hollenback Road at Alum Creek State Park in Delaware County was adventure travel.

Built with state money, donations and thousands of hours of volunteer labor, it was recently named one of the best dog parks in the nation by *Dog Fancy* magazine.

Mickey knew something was up when we turned the wrong way leaving the neighborhood. I can't get the dog too excited because she expresses herself by peeing, so I had to put a dropcloth under her and murmur constant reassurance.

(She also races to her food bowl and eats when I run the vacuum cleaner, but that's another story.)

The free, public dog park, open about a year, has been attracting big canine crowds on weekends. To avoid the canine masses, we went on a weekday evening.

Mickey loves people—when someone visits, we have to put her in her cage for half an hour to take the edge off her hospitality.

But she doesn't especially like dogs.

Oh, she's not hostile—she'll give them a sniff for politeness' sake—but she'd really rather not be bothered socializing with them.

The dog-park crowd was light, but it doesn't take many dogs to annoy Mickey. There was a playful boxer, a couple of Italian greyhounds, the inevitable golden retrievers, a German shepherd, a setter in a life jacket (he was swimming).

All had to say hello. Repeatedly.

Mickey's stance said: "Nice to meet you, too, Rover, but haven't you ever seen a dog before?"

We hung for a while at the beach, with its little waves, because Mickey likes to bark at moving water. I guess it's a vestige from her younger days, when she enjoyed attacking the lawn sprinkler.

She'll still do that but with less abandon, owing to her sight. Her eyes are clouded by cataracts, and for a while she bumped into things. But she has adapted to the point that she navigates the house and backyard without incident.

She's also diabetic, another condition she has adapted to well. The insulin shots are no big deal—the dog will do anything for Pup-Peroni.

I didn't let Mickey run free in the park's fenced areas (separate pens for big and small dogs), not because of her sight but because she'd go straight to the nearest person and make a pest of herself.

Granted, you expect dog-tolerant people at a dog park, but there also seems to be an unspoken courtesy code in effect. People constantly called out—"Roadie!" "Lulu!" "Charlie!"—as their dogs raced to investigate human and canine newcomers.

Mickey was content to walk to and fro, smelling things, peeing on trees, nibbling on grass.

Dog business, in other words. But she did it with more energy than I'd seen out of her in a year.

I knew what she was thinking: Wow, if this place had Milk Bones and some toilet-bowl water, it would be heaven.

Or maybe even the vet's office.

FAREWELL TO MICKEY, THE MEMORABLE POODLE

Jan. 8, 2009

Every pet represents a chapter in a family's life.

A chapter ended in ours last weekend.

Mickey the poodle—who allowed a certain columnist to dress her as a cow, reveal her vacuum-cleaner anxieties and disclose her lack of bladder control—has died.

Let it be known that she was much more than a comic device. She was a family member, and her departure has left us grieving and out of rhythm. I can't even remember to take my cholesterol medication, because my pill schedule was coordinated with hers.

She came to us 12 years ago as a puppy, all black curls and wiggling enthusiasm. For uncertain medical reasons, she was leaky from the start. But we coped by giving her drugs for incontinence and establishing forbidden zones.

(She knew that we, the bringers of Milk-Bones, descended from above every morning, but she was never on the second floor. She thought of it as heaven, where the gods dwelled.)

The outdoors was less easily restricted. She regularly escaped, usually emerging on the next street to the north. We once found her in someone's garage, eating cat food. It was an odd way to meet neighbors.

I've always thought that a key part of the canine mystique is the adorable way they misinterpret our world.

Consider the vacuum cleaner: Where I saw a cleaning device, Mickey saw a rival. Every Saturday morning, I would switch on the Hoover, and Mickey would promptly race to her food bowl to eat. She thought the vacuum woke up for the express purpose of stealing her Dog Chow.

Her trust was strong. She would endure any indignity, from baths to modeling (the aforementioned cow costume), if we ordained it.

The chapter that ended with her passing would have to be titled "Celia's Childhood." Celia, my 18-year-old daughter, was 6 when Mickey arrived, and their bond was deep. As the dog aged, I found myself dreading the day they would have to part.

Mickey's medical infirmities began with diabetes. (She had insulin shots, followed by a Pup-Peroni chaser, twice a day.) Then she went blind. Then she developed seizures, the worst of which landed her in MedVet, the excellent Worthington pet emergency hospital, on the Saturday before Christmas.

She walked out about 30 hours and $1,700 later. I was always one of those people who clucked with disapproval at the resources lavished on pets. So much for that opinion.

The money bought her a pretty good two weeks—little pain, lots of Pup-Peroni—until the end came early Sunday with devastating seizures.

It was Celia who finally said it out loud: We can't let her suffer.

My daughter held Mickey on her lap as the euthanasia drugs were administered. Having participated in the decision, she wasn't going to leave her dog to face the consequences alone. It was the act of an adult. I think I saw two transitions that night.

Since then, everything we do around the house reminds us of Mickey: peel a carrot (she loved carrots), open the back door, pass her nap spot in the middle of the kitchen floor.

A family chapter has ended, but the family is finding it difficult to turn the page.

IT'S TIME FOR DAUGHTER TO FLY THE NEST

July 9, 2009

I thought my daughter would never learn to swim.

She wailed; she clung; she refused to put her head in the water—until one day, at age 5 or so, she decided that she would. And that was that: She swam.

Celia has always done things when she was ready. If she wasn't ready, no amount of cajoling could make her so. She liked to operate on her own terms.

She wore either a hat or a bandanna every waking moment from about age 4 until well into elementary school. We have school photos in which she looks like a member of the Harley-Davidson Junior Auxiliary.

We didn't know whether it was a security device or a fashion statement, but we didn't fight it. We knew she would dispense with the headgear when she was ready. And one day, she was.

I say this to explain why I am less emotional than I expected to be about the fact that Celia, our second and last child, graduated from high school on Sunday. She was ready, eager, itching to graduate. It's hard to be sad when a child is happy.

For the moment, put me down as calm with occasional bouts of wistfulness.

Most of the fun I've had in the past 25 years has involved doing whatever the kids were doing: T-ball, Boy Scouts, church mission trips, band. So, yes, I will miss all that when, come fall, Celia heads off to Ohio State University and my wife and I become empty nesters.

On the other hand, raising a child to be ready for independence is sort of the point of parenthood. I do wish I knew exactly how we did it, though, because I'd write a book.

When parenthood began, I thought of it as a straightforward process that would succeed if my wife and I provided the correct input. I thought we were in control.

But, looking back, I see it as more like a mysterious alchemy in which, somehow, the influence of countless people—parents, relatives, friends, peers, coaches, teachers, ministers—combines with the child herself to form the person she becomes.

I suppose that's how two introverts produced an extrovert. By the third grade, she had a more active social life than I did. Also, she's a good musician in a house where no one else ever picked up an instrument. How do these things happen?

I don't know.

Some people like to use gardening as a metaphor for parenthood. You know: nurturing the seedling and all that. I'd advise new parents to forget that metaphor in a hurry.

In gardening, if you plant a marigold, you get a marigold. In parenting, you never know what kind of exotic flower you might be raising.

We got a skeptical, funny, sociable specimen with an independent streak and a finely tuned social conscience. She still doesn't just jump into things because we, or anyone else, said to. That looks more like an asset now than it did when she was 3.

She's not sure what kind of career she will pursue, but I suspect she will, one way or another, want to express her thoughts on the things that vex her about the world. When she's ready, I imagine that the world will know it.

LES WAS MUCH MORE THAN A FATHER-IN-LAW

May 18, 2004

I've been lucky in the dad department.

In a world in which too many kids don't have even one, I had two: my own and the dad I acquired by marriage.

When my father died in 1981, one of the consolations was that I still had Les Robinson.

The first time I saw him was at the Downtown Greyhound station in 1975. He had come to pick up his daughter and her shaggy-haired boyfriend—an aspiring journalist, of all things.

Les, a conservative man (he didn't wear short pants in public until the late 1960s), wasn't fond of long hair or the media.

But he was a relentless optimist with a generous spirit. He figured I'd work out.

I come from a family that tended to be operatic in its approach to problems. When a pipe broke or a radiator overheated, much vocalizing and lamenting followed.

My second dad, on the other hand, had an irrepressible urge to fix things. His wife, Barbara, remembers that once, in a vacation cabin in Indiana, he encountered a light switch that wasn't working.

So he took it apart. This was on their honeymoon.

As a young man, he became a partner in an engineering firm, but he had a long-standing goal of becoming financially independent through real estate. I recall an old rental house with a ramshackle garage he bought in Westerville in the late 1970s.

"Burn it down" was my thought when I saw the garage. But Dad had a plan: I would stand inside the structure while he drove his van slowly into the bowed-out back wall. When the wall was plumb, we would nail it fast.

I was only mildly concerned that the garage would collapse on me.

Dad's ideas were sometimes unorthodox but always sound. The garage looked much better after he'd collided with it.

He and Barb became Dad and Mom to me early on. When I struggled to find a job in journalism in our first year of marriage, they wouldn't let me give up.

Finally, I landed one—in part because Barb called the editor of the *Parkersburg Sentinel* in West Virginia and told him he should hire me. He did.

Dad reached his career goals, too: He left engineering in his mid-50s for real estate. But this was no land baron out to impress the world. He called himself a maintenance man and dressed the part.

His Palm Pilot was a pocket calendar with a stub of pencil clipped on it. He reused tea bags.

I've lived in three houses in central Ohio; each bore his marks. There was no better sight than to see him at the door, 5-gallon bucket full of tools in hand, ready to tackle some project that had me baffled.

He had an almost-exasperating sense of self-reliance. When his health began to fail, doctors would give him detailed diagnoses of his pancreatic, liver and lung problems. And he'd tell them he needed to get out and walk more.

Illness slowed but couldn't stop him. He and Mom traveled.

He began sculpting with clay. He threw himself into intense Bible study.

He played with his grandchildren (they called him Pops), who adored him because he'd take them to the basement and spend hours building little things that were never finished.

He died last week, just 73 years old. I learned so much from him that I like to think he raised three children—and a son-in-law.

BAD BREAK HAD ITS GOOD RESULTS

August 10, 2010

To reiterate: I broke my right elbow falling off a bicycle six weeks ago. Too bad, but in every fracture there is a silver lining.

And so I present Eight Pretty Good Outcomes from a Broken Elbow:

1. My daughter cut the grass all summer.

2. I discovered I could floss my teeth one-handed if I tied one end to a cabinet handle and held the other end in my left hand.

By the way, when held taut, a length of floss twangs like a guitar string. If you ever see me using dental twine to play "Oh! Susanna" on *America's Got Talent*, you'll know how I discovered the technique.

3. I got a glimpse into the future.

Having to do everything left-handed slowed me down to half-speed on chores such as weeding the garden or taking out the trash. I'm guessing that will be my pace in about 25 years (if I'm lucky).

This tells me that the house will, at some point, become way too big.

4. I realized that my odd mixture of right- and left-handedness has advantages.

I'm right-handed, but I've always done a few things (throwing a ball, for example) with my left. I've sometimes wondered whether that was a physical expression of a deep-seated psychological ambivalence that Woody Allen's therapist could help me sort out.

Turns out it was simply preparation for the day I would have to eat soup left-handed. My left hand caught on fast.

5. I might have gained a little protection from Alzheimer's disease.

Using your non-dominant hand is supposedly good for brain health. I don't know whether I believe it. But, if I can still remember all of the grandkids' names at 89, I will attribute it to my elbow. It will make a good story, at least.

6. I finally watched *The Wire.*

Forced onto the couch, I managed to get through three seasons' worth of that HBO show on DVD. And what a show.

I still can't believe they killed—well, I won't spoil it.

Surely, I'm not the only person who runs seven years behind in TV viewing.

Incidentally, has anyone else noticed how many acclaimed cable dramas (*The Sopranos, The Wire, Weeds, Big Love, Nurse Jackie*) revolve around people who try to carry on normal lives while living outside the law? I'd say it's a formula.

7. I enjoyed the blessings of modern medicine.

I would have enjoyed them more if I didn't feel just a little guilty about the resources lavished on my elbow. It probably cost $25,000 (paid mostly by the insurer) to fix it.

That's more than it costs to send a kid to a state college for a year. Had I not been insured, I would probably have had to ask whether I could afford to regain full use of my arm. A lot of people in this economy probably do have to ask that type of question. That's sad.

8. I was reminded of how nonchalantly a certain young woman and I repeated that phrase "in sickness and in health" 35 years ago.

Time and the occasional broken bone have taught me how lucky I am that she hasn't forgotten the promise.

DANCING MIGHT NOT MAKE HIM A STAR

Sept. 30, 2010

I've been taking dance lessons.

To be precise, I've taken three dance lessons. So can I dance? Yes, with about the same level of skill that I could transplant a heart after three lessons.

The impetus for this little adventure is my son's impending wedding.

Being parents of the groom, my wife and I figured we couldn't execute the usual wedding dance strategy: Wait until the floor gets crowded, then hide behind intoxicated people.

Therefore, we bought the $59 two-lesson introductory package at Dance Plus Ballroom in Grandview Heights.

When it became apparent that two lessons wouldn't quite do it, we added a third. Then we considered hiring Neil Duncan, our instructor, to come to the wedding, stand near us and whisper left-right-slow-slow-fast-fast.

Actually, Neil, a miracle-worker, had us making progress at the studio. The problem was that, on the drive home, we would promptly forget everything we learned.

I began dancing my fingers in the car to preserve the precious knowledge we had just acquired. I'm actually better at the finger fox trot than the real one.

We got little encouragement at home. Our 19-year-old daughter was horrified by the whole idea of her parents dancing. When we returned from the first lesson, I said, "Hey, want to watch us waltz?"

She fled the room, as if I'd said, "Hey, want to watch us make out?"

The dance package also entitled us to attend a few dance parties. But they included a tricky element: music. I know it tends to be an essential part of the activity, but music distracted me from counting one-two-three, one-two-three.

My wife, bless her heart, has been very patient, and I've made a determined effort not to injure her. Still, tensions arise. Ballroom dancing isn't quite as hard on a marriage as, say, loading a dishwasher, but it does carry a risk of agitation.

I, for example, had a tendency to hold her hands too tightly. She would point out that it's difficult to execute a twirl when I'm grasping her fingers like a rock-climber clutching a granite ledge.

Then I would point out that I had four limbs and couldn't be expected to keep an eye on all of them, especially when my feet required near constant vigilance.

Nevertheless, we've made it through entire songs with scarcely a cross word. Granted, that doesn't make either of us a Rockette, but I think it shows glimmers of competence.

I've read that dancing is a very healthful activity. It forces the brain to make new connections, improving memory and cognition.

I see a certain Catch-22 in that proposition: Dancing will improve my memory, but only if I can remember the dance steps first.

I'm working on it. But I think the evening will be unforgettable whether I forget the box step or not.

A SON'S WEDDING, A DAD'S BLESSINGS

Oct. 14, 2010

Noah Blundo and Elizabeth Goussetis were married in an afternoon ceremony Saturday in the Annunciation Greek Orthodox Cathedral.

The bride is the daughter of Harry and Amy Goussetis of the Westerville area. The groom is the son of Joe and Deborah Blundo of Worthington.

The bride wore an ivory wedding gown. The groom wore a black tuxedo. The groom's dad wore a dazed expression.

Having all those people from different stages of a couple's life appear in one place reminded him of a dream. Except in a dream, he would discover that he'd forgotten to wear pants.

It was, of course, impossible for the groom's dad to watch his 27-year-old son get married without seeing the 7-month-old and the 7-year-old he once was.

Having the groom dressed up in a formal setting brought back memories of when he served in a Cub Scout color guard for Vice President Al Gore and thought it would be a breach of decorum if he scratched his nose.

The groom was considerably more relaxed on this occasion, as was the bride. In fact, she was bouncing a little on the altar.

The groom's dad has seen gowns that wore brides, essentially submerging them in swaths of fabric. Not this bride. She was as comfortable and animated in her gown as Kristi Yamaguchi is in a skating outfit.

The bride was escorted down the aisle by her father.

The groom's dad had lighter responsibilities. He had to escort the groom's mom without tripping. He had to greet guests in the reception line. And he had to make sure that the pastries for the wedding-reception cookie table (an Italian-American tradition) got delivered.

If you wanted to measure a family's enthusiasm for a wedding in sugar, butter and flour, 250 cookies would be mildly interested, and 500 would be excited. The groom's dad's relatives baked about 1,000. They were off-the-cookie-charts excited.

The ceremony was followed by a reception in the church social hall, at which there was Greek dancing, Italian dancing and whatever you call it when the groom's dad attempts to bust a move.

The groom's dad and probably every other guest of his generation nursed sore knees and sore feet (along with other afflictions) the next day. Joint pain: the mark of a good wedding.

For the record, the groom's dad didn't need to dab his eyes with a handkerchief a single time during the event. Why? He was watching two people he loves get married in the presence of dozens of other people he loves. What's to cry about?

Of course, it takes the groom's dad a while to process things. So later, yes, he got teary-eyed when he reflected on the fact that the bride and groom had included, in the wedding program, a tribute to their grandparents who didn't live to see the day.

Reading his own parents' names in the program got to the groom's dad. So did the idea that this young couple had the sensitivity to include them.

The newlyweds planned a honeymoon trip to Costa Rica.

The groom's dad will stay home and count his blessings.

'MOM' WAS MORE THAN A MOTHER-IN-LAW

June 2, 2011

In 1976, I was a discouraged college graduate, pretty sure that I would never get to use my journalism degree at a newspaper.

Barbara Ann Robinson didn't share my pessimism.

She had been my mother-in-law for just a few months, but she already had more confidence in me than I had in myself. And she wasn't shy about expressing it.

So, on a visit to her hometown of Parkersburg, W.Va., she called the editor of the *Parkersburg Sentinel* (whom she didn't know) and told him he should give me a job interview.

She must have left an impression because, when I called the editor myself, he remembered her. Two months later, I was a reporter for his newspaper. If you want to blame someone for these columns I write three times a week, blame Barb Robinson.

My mother-in-law—whom I always called Mom—died Sunday at age 76.

She was a woman of strong preferences. She favored Republicans; Jimmy Dean breakfast sandwiches; and, in her younger days, slot machines. We still have some little bottles of shampoo from the Golden Nugget in Las Vegas.

I wed her daughter when I was 21—too dumb to have even considered the idea that, when you marry someone, you also marry her family. I was just lucky to have chosen a good one.

Mom was trained as a nurse, and she was good at it. She and her husband, Les, once cut short a trip and drove 900 miles back to Columbus because I needed an appendectomy and she was going to be there to make sure that it went well.

Later, they entered the rental real-estate business. Every Labor Day weekend, I'd show up at their campus-area apartments to help get them ready for a fresh crop of none-too-gentle college students. (The kids who ignited a charcoal grill in the living room stand out in memory.)

She could be hell on a tenant who left her torn window screens or a dirty stove. It violated her sense of fair play.

But, for people who needed help, she couldn't do enough. She moved a family of immigrants into one of her apartments at a ridiculously low rent because she wanted to help them get settled here.

She and Les, who died in 2004, reminded me of my own parents, in that people thought of them as a unit. They did everything together: work, travel, spoil the grandchildren. The kids called them Meme and Pops.

A few weeks ago, Mom got the disturbing results of some medical tests: She had several aneurysms in her brain. Her choices were to do nothing—which would have meant continued decline—or undergo a procedure that could fix the problem but carried significant risk.

She chose to take the risk. I wasn't surprised. She had developed a strong faith. And she knew how to be bold when it counted.

On the night before the procedure, I went to see her. She was groggy and a little anxious, but she introduced me to a nurse the way she often did: "This is my son-in-law. But he's really more like a son." That's one of the last things I ever heard her say.

Rest in peace, Mom.

NEW GRADUATE GETS HERSELF NOTICED

May 7, 2013

Sure, the president was there, but the most exciting moment during the Ohio State University commencement on Sunday occurred when my daughter, Celia, got up to go to the bathroom.

She was one of 8,000 or so graduates in identical gowns at Ohio Stadium—so, from our perspective, the restroom break allowed her to rise from anonymity. (Students receiving undergraduate degrees don't cross a stage or have their names announced, because that would take hours.)

A sharp-eyed aunt spotted her, and a flurry of excitement ensued in our row.

A few other spectators must have thought, "Wow, those people are easily entertained." But who could blame us?

That was our baby out there getting a college diploma. She represented the attainment of goals, the fulfillment of dreams and—not insignificantly—the end of the Tuition Era.

Both kids have college degrees—which satisfies me and puts me in a reflective frame of mind.

So I'd like to thank their great-grandparents for immigrating here a century ago. I'd also like to thank whoever dreamed up the GI Bill, so my dad, a veteran, could buy a house and join the middle class—and the taxpayers of not just the school district that educated my kids but also the school districts that educated everyone in their lives who guided them.

As President Barack Obama said in his commencement speech: "We are not a collection of strangers; we are bound to one another by a set of ideals and laws and commitments."

I don't think the woman sitting behind me heard him; she was too busy muttering disdainfully at every comment he made.

The Class of 2013 will see plenty of entertaining political campaigns, I suspect.

The member of the class who drew me to Ohio Stadium is moving on to graduate school—to study screenwriting at DePaul University in Chicago. When I tell other people, they aren't sure what to make of that, because, in terms of employability, screenwriting isn't exactly software engineering.

Celia, though, sees a world badly in need of satirizing (yes, it could be in the genes), and I'm pleased to see her accept the mission.

Obama did say to dream big, after all.

She'll write big, too, if her blog is any indication. I've been known to say that, if her grandmothers weren't dead, some of what she has written would probably kill them. But a writer has to say what is on her mind.

Her influences include *The Simpsons* (she drew a portrait of Homer on her mortarboard), Tina Fey, David Sedaris and other smartasses too numerous to mention. She loves to skewer conservatives, consumerism and *Cosmopolitan* sex advice.

She'll enter Chicago the same way she entered Ohio Stadium: as another face in the crowd. But we'll watch intently for signs that she's on the rise.

That's our baby out there.

TURNING 60 A CHANCE TO DENY, DENY, DENY

April 17, 2014

Five words come to mind when I contemplate turning 60 today: There must be some mistake.

From time to time during the past few weeks, I've actually subtracted 1954 from 2014 just to double-check the math.

True, I have some of the markers of 60: graying hair, grown children, instant recall of *I Love Lucy* episodes.

But I also continue to harbor childhood fantasies and adolescent knowledge deficits. (I still don't know how to balance a checkbook.)

Maybe life should send me back a decade or two for more training.

I laughed off entering my 50s, but I have to admit that entering my 60s seems more serious.

It is, after all, the decade when the Social Security Administration begins paying you for being old. That kind of makes it official.

It would probably be easier to fathom the idea of turning 60 if I were from a less delusional generation.

Baby boomers are famous for pretending they can defy the laws of aging (with a little help from Botox, plastic surgery and erectile-dysfunction drugs).

Being a boomer, I am supposed to claim that, at 60, I am just as robust and vigorous as ever.

And that might even be true—on a good day before 9:30 p.m.

But I have devised a more nuanced form of denial in recognition of the fact that body parts don't seem to age at the same rate.

When the alarm clock rings in the morning, I do a quick survey of body parts and assign each an age.

On Tuesday, for example, my left shoulder—which has been hurting recently—felt 60. But my knees were more like 52, and my right earlobe was not a day older than 35. Averaging these numbers meant I could spring out of bed at an age of 49.

Hey, anything to gain an edge.

As I stand on this age plateau, I am at once deeply grateful for having arrived in pretty good health and acutely aware of how quickly that could disappear. No one lives six decades without life teaching that there are no guarantees.

I don't obsess over the risk of illness, but I do keep my ears open for health strategies.

Recently, I've been fascinated by research that found a correlation between longevity and the ability to rise from the floor without grabbing onto something or using a hand or knee for support. (Getting off the floor seems a good skill at any age. It would have been useful at some college parties.)

The research didn't say that practicing the unassisted floor rise would make you live longer, but I've been practicing anyway.

If nothing else, it might make an entertaining parlor trick when all of us ageless baby boomers need some fun in the nursing home.

GRANDPA CELEBRATING 7 POUNDS OF HOPE

Aug. 10, 2017

Andreas Benjamin Blundo, bearing a nice head of hair and the names of two great-grandfathers, arrived at 8:43 p.m. on Aug. 5.

I am now a grandparent. (The full title is "surprisingly youthful grandparent," but we can dispense with formalities.)

People have been telling me for months that I will love being a grandparent, and I must say, the first few days have been great. His parents care for the child, and I stand around adoring him. It's a lovely arrangement.

For many months, I tried to hold back the flood of hopes for this first grandchild because one learns not to be too presumptuous in life. Things happen.

But now that he's finally here, I permit myself some dreaming. Eventually, I might anticipate soccer goals and piano recitals, but right now, I look forward to simpler experiences.

I want him to ask me a million questions, such as why is the grass green and are there any fish in that puddle over there. We'll go out and get dirty looking for answers.

I want to hear the results when his busy little brain puzzles out the complexities of language and he confidently declares something such as: "Owls wake up at night and eat mouses." (My daughter blurted that out at age 3; it remains one of my favorite scientific observations.)

I want to watch him develop a sense of self and throw epic tantrums in defense of it. As a parent, it took me awhile to appreciate tantrums as just another stage of development, but once I did, they became entertaining.

I want to make him laugh uncontrollably because there's no audience better than a toddler who sees the humor in a man putting stuffed animals on his head.

Even though I was lucky enough to be present for just about everything my kids did, parenthood still went by in a blur. I was keenly aware of that—in your 60s, wistfulness ramps up—late last year when my son Noah and daughter-in-law Elizabeth had a family dinner and sprang the big news by handing out name tags. Mine said "Grandpa."

Talk about hitting the reset button.

The new title sounded wonderful in theory, but I couldn't fully appreciate its impact until I walked into room 5213 at OhioHealth Riverside Methodist Hospital on Saturday night and felt the gravitational pull from a 7-pound, 4-ounce boy in a diaper.

For most of Sunday, we let the new parents and their infant catch up on sleep as best they could. I went out and played softball for a few hours. When I returned home, my wife said "Hello." I said, "Let's go see our baby."

ON THE SCENE

HE FLIES THROUGH THE AIR WITH THE GREATEST UNEASE

April 10, 2005

Come fly with Peter Pan, a publicist said.

OK, I said, reasoning that in this litigious age there would be no actual flying, just dangling.

I hate airplanes and roller coasters, but hanging from a cable like a beef carcass I can handle.

So I went to the Palace Theatre, where Cathy Rigby is starring in *Peter Pan*. And there was Rigby herself, the actress and ex-gymnast who is making her last tour as Peter Pan after nearly 20 years of cable-assisted levitation.

She quickly picked up on my unease about flying and wryly exploited it.

"Yes, it's always gone well," she said of her aerial experiences onstage, "except for the few times it didn't."

I was to be the third flier, giving me, oh, I'd say about an eternity to contemplate the adventure. Preceding me were Anne Allred of WSYX (Channel 6)—who, like me, was flying on business—and Lara Baker of Worthington, who won a flight in a drawing.

"I'm a little nervous," Baker said.

Intellectually, I knew that the stunt had to be ultra-safe. Baker, after all, is chief legal counsel for the Columbus city attorney. The Palace wouldn't want to risk dropping a lawyer.

But what keeps me off airplanes and roller coasters is emotion, not intellect. And my vision of a tame hovering experience quickly evaporated when I watched Allred, then Baker, suddenly ascend into the lights and swoop across the stage at an impressive altitude.

"Whoa, Mom," Baker's 3-year-old son, Sam, yelled from the audience. "Look at you!"

She was traversing the stage while hanging from an alarmingly slender cable.

"It's one-sixteenth-inch aircraft cable," said Paul Rubin, the show's aerial expert.

"Can't we get some one-eighth in here?" I asked.

Not to worry, he said: The cable will hold 1,000 pounds. Funny, that's about how much dread I was carrying.

The cable is attached to a system of ropes and pulleys that Rubin and his colleague Randy Rees control. They send Rigby, a veteran of more than 2,600 *Peter Pan* performances, soaring and dipping at high speed.

"Sometimes, when Cathy's flying, she reaches two G's," Rubin said.

Yes, but she gets paid more than I do.

After signing a waiver that mentioned "personal injury or death," I was strapped into the harness.

You get into some strange situations in this business. Here I was, cinched and tethered, with Cathy Rigby sprinkling "fairy dust" and telling me to close my eyes and think "lovely thoughts."

Instead, I squinted and contemplated my mortality.

Then Rubin and Rees went into action, and I was 20 feet in the air before I knew it. They swung me to and fro across the stage while I tried to look graceful.

"Arch your back," Rigby called from below. "Bend your knees."

I found both unnecessary. The panicked swimming motions seemed to be amusing onlookers perfectly well.

"Do you like roller coasters?" Rubin asked.

"No," I said, too late to stop him from putting me through a "death-drop" finale before I returned gratefully to Earth.

Well, it was interesting. I left feeling a kinship with Rigby. She makes stage flying look easy. I make it look hard.

POT ROAST NO MATCH FOR DELICACY OF DANVILLE

Feb. 11, 2007

If ever there seemed a formula for low attendance, it was this: brutal cold outside and 500 pounds of roasting raccoon inside.

But Danville, 50 miles northeast of Columbus in Knox County, loves its Raccoon Dinner.

People braved the subzero wind chill, some lining up 15 minutes early at St. Luke Community Center for the 63rd annual event last week.

But raccoon? Really?

I went thinking it would be like a turkey shoot where they don't really shoot turkeys.

Not so. This was the real thing—21 big, electric roasting pans of raccoon. And, no, it doesn't taste like chicken.

The analogy I've heard most often is that raccoon a la Danville approximates the taste of a tender pot roast.

I find that comparison lacking. Raccoon meat is richer, moister, more intense. It's extreme pot roast.

"It's unique, but it's really good," said Holly Hofacker, an 18-year-old first-timer from St. Louisville.

She came with Dustin Sherman, 17, of Utica. He's a dinner veteran so sold on the worthiness of raccoon that he felt secure inviting her.

She had seconds, which must bode well for their friendship.

Danville has had six decades to perfect the art of turning a tough varmint into a tender entree.

The dinner was founded by a small circle of hunters who took turns hosting it in their homes. For a long time it was male-only, said head cook Barb Mickley, whose father-in-law was one of the hunters.

She finally laid down the law: "I told my father-in-law, 'I'm not working anymore if I can't eat.'"

Now it's a family event that draws about 600 people. The dinner raises $1,500 to $2,000 annually for the sponsoring Lions Club, according to club President Sandra Crow.

Woody Hayes and Gov. James A. Rhodes have been among the after-dinner speakers. This year it was Bill Conley, a former Ohio State assistant football coach and recruiting coordinator.

The 207 raccoons on the menu were bagged between mid-November and the end of January, then frozen.

"I've been catching coon for the coon supper since I was 7 or 8 years old," said Leonard Mickley, 52-year-old nephew of Barb. Mickley and his nephew, Brian Payne, supplied about half the meat this year.

"We do it for fun and to help the farmers out," Mickley said. "Raccoons are a pest."

The day before each dinner, the meat is thawed, soaked in salt water and distributed to volunteers. They brown it at home and take it to the church hall for three hours of roasting with onions and garlic.

A couple of Dublin police officers, Jeff Hall and John Kreuz, drove an hour to sample the results.

Hall, a Danville native who hadn't been to a dinner in 25 years, said it tasted just as he remembered. Kreuz, a novice, also gave good reviews.

"I was expecting something real greasy—and I'd have to get a chain saw out to cut it—but it's real tender."

Others were less enthusiastic.

"I feel like I'm eating roadkill," said Shelly Gonzales, 15, of Danville. "It didn't taste bad. It's just weird to think about."

Farmer David Hawk, 35, also passed up a chance to dine on creatures that might well have dined on his crops.

"I see them in the fields all the time, and I'm just not interested in eating them," he said.

He had ham, an alternative offered to the raccoon-resistant. There were few takers but still too many to suit Barb Mickley.

"If I had my say, I wouldn't even serve anything else. This is a raccoon dinner."

HE CAME, HE SAW, HE SCULPTED AN ORANGE FISH

Feb. 15, 2007

A new exhibit at the Wexner Center for the Arts features a sculpture of startling creativity.

Its innovative interpretation of form and bold use of color hint at a restless need to defy convention.

The piece fairly crackles with the tension between attractiveness and repulsion—making a sly comment on the duality of existence and challenging assumptions.

Unless someone has smushed my masterpiece already.

When I heard that the center was opening an exhibit that allows visitors to mold colorful blocks of clay, I hurried there on opening day.

How many opportunities do I get to display preschool-quality sculpture under museum-quality lighting at Ohio State University?

"Charles Long: 100 lbs. of Clay" consists of 100 colorful blocks of the stuff, each on its own little shelf. Visitors take it from there.

By the time I arrived, some blocks already resembled certain body parts. Clearly, the OSU student population had been at work.

Other forms also caught my eye: a hand holding a business card, a braided spider, the inevitable Block O. (It collapsed while I watched—which I took as a metaphor for the national-title game.)

The sight of all this handwork can be a little intimidating. You see, anyone can squash anyone else's sculpture and fashion it into something new. This seems a little like kicking your buddy's building-block tower in kindergarten.

And which one to destroy: the red flower, the vaguely obscene cylinder, the blue crucifix?

Fortunately, physics resolved my problem. Someone's orange blob fell off its pedestal and practically rolled to my feet, begging to be reworked.

For inspiration, I harked back to my days of sculpting Play-Doh with the kids. My default subject then was a fish. It's an easy shape to make but less predictable than a snake. (I've always been conscious of how my art will be received by critics.)

This being the Wexner Center, I thought the fish should offer an alternative vision that re-imagines stereotypical forms and conflates gracefulness with crudity (because critics always appreciate an excuse to use the word conflate).

So I gave the fish horns, a gaping mouth, winglike fins, an eyeless face and a dismayingly long tongue.

Others might have overworked the piece, but I left it rough. Was I making a witty comment on the innocence of folk art or just bumping against the limits of my Play-Doh technique?

When finished, I placed my orange masterpiece on a high shelf. There it would be visible to discerning patrons descending a stairway nearby, yet out of reach of second-graders who might turn it into a pumpkin.

My strategy worked: The sculpture survived awhile—unlike the crucifix (not that you should read too much into that).

I'm tempted to say it belongs to the ages. But I suspect that it really belongs to any artist tall enough to snatch it off the shelf.

CLOSE SHAVE PAMPERS PLEBIAN LIKE A KING

July 19, 2007

You've seen my face, so I won't try to argue that it deserves a shave worthy of British royalty.

Most mornings, I just run an electric razor over it—the way a farmer runs a Bush Hog over scrubland.

But when I heard there's a place in Columbus that charges up to $60 for a shave of kings, I had to try it.

John Bowman calls his place Studio 997. It rests amid modest houses on Sells Avenue, near Ohio State University's West Campus.

Bowman, 60, has a head of gray hair, thin on top but well-cut. His Vandyke beard has precise curves and crisp edges. His studio has a simple, pleasing decor and good views from its many windows.

You want to see such attention to detail when a man is proposing to wield a straight razor near your jugular vein.

Early in his career, Bowman cut hair at the Neil House, the long-gone Broad-and-High hotel where visiting celebrities and politicians stayed. He once turned down a chance to barber Cary Grant.

(The actor wanted a haircut in his room; Bowman told him to come to the barbershop. Grant did, but, by then, Bowman was gone; someone else did the honors.)

These days, Bowman distinguishes himself from other hairdressers by proclaiming his affiliation with Britain's Truefitt & Hill, reputedly the oldest barbershop in the world and the official pruners of the male side of the royal family.

About a year ago, Bowman was trained in "master shaving" techniques by the Truefitt & Hill branch in Las Vegas and now practices them here.

He has an upscale clientele of regulars, plus guys who come bearing gift certificates from their wives, plus occasional groups that book him for "shaving parties" in the garden behind his shop.

Various services are available. I opted for the $30 shave, which takes a half-hour and involves nine hot towels, glycerin-laden shave cream, several essential oils, moisturizers and a neck massage.

For another $30, I could have had the shave plus a facial with exfoliants, cleansers and the application of 200 million-year-old Australian mud to eliminate toxins. (You'd think mud in which dinosaurs could have wallowed would *contribute* toxins, but what do I know?)

"I'm not selling the shave; I'm selling the experience," Bowman said as we began.

He lowers the lights, plays classical music and speaks softly during the process.

"Some of my clients go to sleep with the first towel," he said.

I stayed awake because it's not often that I recline under hot towels like a Mafia kingpin.

It was an aromatic event, with various woodsy, herbal potions applied to soften, moisturize and otherwise anoint my face between sessions with the razor.

I felt pretty well-shaved after the first pass with the blade, but then Bowman did a second pass against the grain—not unlike the double-cutting they do on the fairways at Muirfield Village Golf Club, I imagine.

This resulted in an extremely close shave that left me feeling groomed and refreshed, and I kept glancing in the mirror to make sure I hadn't accidentally picked up someone else's chin.

I still don't look like Prince William, but there's only so much a master shaver can do.

RIDE IN $2 MILLION BUGATTI LEAVES HIM BUG-EYED

July 10, 2012

John Hill knew that I wasn't a prospective Bugatti buyer, but any lingering doubt would have been removed when I asked how much the handmade tires cost.

"When I'm talking to a potential buyer, if they raise that issue, you know they're not going to buy," Hill said.

A set of four tires costs $35,000, by the way. It lasts 6,000 to 8,000 miles.

Hill, who grew up in Worthington and lives in Virginia, is sales director for the North and South American operations of Bugatti, which sent a $2.05 million sports car to the weekend Arthritis Foundation Classic Auto Show and Cruise In.

The typical buyer of such a product, Hill said, is an independently wealthy collector who already owns many exotic cars and appreciates the beauty of precision machinery—emphatically not I, in other words.

But, given my position as a bemused observer of human-consumption habits, I was invited to drive the Bugatti.

I couldn't say no, because how often will I have the chance to risk wrecking something worth more than a New Albany mansion?

Here's my favorite Bugatti fact: The leather interior is made from the hides of cattle pastured high in the Alps so that no insect bites will mar their pristine hides. (Evidently, Bugatti buyers don't have kids—most of whom could ruin $50,000 worth of Alpine leather with one McDonald's ketchup packet.)

Hill took me on a ride around Dublin to give me an idea of the car's power.

We did break 80 mph only for the briefest of moments, but even that left my stomach a quarter-mile behind. It was like a ride in a particle accelerator. I swear I saw a Higgs boson flash by.

We didn't want to test Dublin police vigilance, so you'll have to take Hill's word for these other benchmarks: At 100 mph, the windows automatically roll up to preserve aerodynamics. At 137, a rear spoiler deploys and the car lowers itself by an inch and a half for extra stability. At 253 mph (the car's top speed), the car calls your wife and tells her to make funeral arrangements.

I'm kidding about that last part, but you get the idea. It's a rocket. There's not a lot of engine roar, just a rush of air as the car inhales like Usain Bolt taking in oxygen on his way to an Olympic sprinting record.

When my turn to drive came, I thought mostly about how ridiculous it would be to bankrupt the *Dispatch* by rear-ending a Chevy Suburban in this vehicle. So I was cautious. And, really, there's no need to show off. The mere fact of being seated in the car makes you feel like the queen of the Rose Parade. It's a gawker magnet.

I was content to do 70 in a 65-mph zone and wave at passing cars.

But I can report that the performance is breathtaking. The aluminum-and-carbon-fiber body is perfect. The gas mileage (8 mpg in the city, 16 on the highway) isn't as bad as I thought.

The only flaw I could find is that the car has no cup holders. Drinking a Big Gulp in a $2 million car is simply not done, I suppose. But no cup holders? It was a deal breaker for me.

I'll stick with the 2002 Toyota.

VOLUNTEERS GAIN DIFFERENT IMAGE OF CLEVELAND

June 25, 2013

If you want to really get to know a place, volunteer there.

I'm back from a week of doing that in Cleveland.

For the most part, I was in neither tourist Cleveland (Lake Erie, the Rock and Roll Hall of Fame) nor comedian Cleveland (underachieving sports teams, polka, river fire).

I was in a gritty, working-class Cleveland neighborhood where the daily sights include an international bakery, a community garden, and a barbershop with a hand-lettered sign reading, "Door locked for security."

I was with about 20 adults and high-school students from North Broadway United Methodist Church. When people ask me what I like about the church, I always say, "We do stuff." The annual volunteer trip is, for me, among the most important stuff we do.

In Cleveland, we stayed at the Nehemiah Mission—once a church, now a volunteer base, food pantry and neighborhood magnet. (We played a kickball game with the neighborhood kids that I think had a dozen people in the outfield alone.)

Nehemiah sends volunteers out to hammer and saw some comfort into the lives of people who are struggling to hang on.

On the first morning, we received our assignments: A man whose elderly father has to be carried out of the house by several family members needs a wheelchair ramp; a woman who lost her job needs her collapsing porch repaired; a husband and wife in their 60s with health problems need a rickety basement staircase reinforced.

The list of jobs is longer than the list of volunteers, so homeowners wait a long time for help. Our arrival at the house with the rickety staircase was a cause for celebration.

He was lying in a hospital bed in the living room but greeted us enthusiastically. She was effusive, warm and eager to introduce us to her several cats and show us the backyard garden.

They keep his ancient motorcycle out there as sort of a lawn ornament. Moss was growing out of the seat. He hadn't ridden it since a car making a careless left turn sent him flying to the pavement years ago.

She was holding things together for both of them until her appendix burst a few months ago, necessitating at least two surgeries. Then everything got difficult, and navigating those scary steps to the basement washing machine became a threat.

We spent the entire week fixing them, in part because anything more complicated than hanging a picture is challenging for me and in part because our presence in the house seemed to delight our hosts. We learned about their interests (they like music and photography), their joys (they celebrated their 45th wedding anniversary while we were there) and their sorrows (they lost a son).

We left them with a safer stairway.

They left us with a different image of Cleveland.

HE'S GETTING A BIG HEAD—WITH GOVERNMENT'S OK

Jan. 14, 2014

Yes, that's my giant face on S. 3rd Street.

I'm part of a branding campaign—ironic because I rarely miss a chance to make fun of branding campaigns.

The advertising sign, which hangs on a building just south of the newspaper office at 34 S. 3rd St., encourages you to "Stay cozy with Ohio's best paper."

The rest of the slogan was going to be "or we'll make his face even bigger," but the city graphics commission would probably have nixed that as too many words.

Seriously, the ad had to get the OK of the city officials who make rulings on signs. So my face is government-approved. (I just want to point that out to critics—of which I'm sure there are many—of my face.)

And now I'd like to address questions I'm afraid that people are asking about the ad:

Q: Doesn't *The Dispatch* have any better-looking employees to put on a sign?

A: In fact, we do. They'll appear on future signs in ascending order of attractiveness. That's better than the other way around.

Q: Aren't you concerned that your giant face is a distraction to drivers and, therefore, a safety hazard?

A: Actually, I'm more concerned that motorists will take a detour to avoid it.

For several days now, I've been nervously monitoring traffic volume on 3rd Street to make sure that it doesn't fall below average. If you have no other reason to drive on 3rd, do so to preserve my self-esteem.

Q: Why so bundled up?

A: The original idea was for me to pose in a Speedo on the beach, with the slogan "The Dispatch: Uncovering uncomfortable secrets."

Then we sought the opinions of Victoria's Secret consultants, who know something about optimum skin exposure.

They took one look at me and said, "Dress him in as many clothes as possible."

Q: Do you think this will help or hurt your career?

A: In just a few days, my image has already been transformed from obscure Midwestern columnist to obscure Midwestern columnist in a funny hat. Never underestimate the power of a funny hat.

Q: What's with the mustache? This isn't 1974.

A: As I've explained more than once through the years, my wife has never seen me without a mustache. I don't want to walk into the house clean-shaven and have her ask to see some ID.

Also consider this: The mustache is 40 years old. So it's sort of a historic artifact of the disco era. If I threatened to shave it off now, preservationists might object. And then the authorities would be forced to get involved.

Remember, my face is government-approved.

FOLK STUDIES

PROGNOSIS PUT THINGS IN PERSPECTIVE

Oct. 10, 2006

When things looked grim, Eva Harsh took her children, 6 and 4, to a practice funeral.

It was 1974, and she had breast cancer. She wanted them to be prepared in case the next funeral was hers.

She didn't tell them that her own death might come soon. She just wanted to lessen the shock should it come.

So she called Jerry Spears Funeral Home and got permission to attend the funeral of someone she didn't know.

The kids were so small that she had to lift them to see the deceased in his casket.

"That's a hard step to take when you're a young mother," she said.

Now she is a grandmother. She's healthy, active and fond of saying, "God is good, and life is great."

Aggressive treatment, family support and a sense of humor helped her survive a grave diagnosis 32 years ago. She and her husband, Greg, agreed to talk about the experience because October is Breast Cancer Awareness Month.

Not that they need any reminders.

The Harshes, who live in Pleasant Township, met at Pleasantview High School and were married in 1968.

She was 27 when she felt a lump in her breast one morning while taking a shower. She had a mastectomy a few days after Mother's Day in 1974 and, later, a hysterectomy.

Even with cancer, Mrs. Harsh said, death seemed so inconceivable that she misunderstood when her doctor said she would probably be on chemotherapy for the rest of her life.

"I said, 'You mean 30 or 40 years?'"

He didn't mean even that many months.

At one of her low points after surgery, she asked her husband whether he wanted a divorce. He took her in his arms and said, "If I lost my leg, would you divorce me?"

Mrs. Harsh said it took at least five years for her to feel normal again. Exercise helped. So did her mother, who cared for her and the children while Mr. Harsh, a truck driver, was at work. She pushed Mrs. Harsh the way only a mother can.

"I was laying on the couch, and she let me know that she thought it was time I started helping with the dishes again."

Looking back three decades later, Mrs. Harsh said she's grateful that her doctor, Tom F. Lewis, prescribed aggressive surgery. She said she would tell women not to rule it out. The lost body parts seem a small price to pay.

"You can hide it," she has told other women facing similar surgery. "You can still put on a pretty blouse and go dancing."

Her husband has his own way of expressing it.

"I don't mean to sound callous about it, but it's not that important. So she's missing a part of her. So what?"

Today, Mrs. Harsh is an upbeat 58-year-old who works at the Delphi auto-parts plant and looks forward to seeing her two grandchildren. She still has a mammogram every year, noting ruefully that she doesn't get a discount for only one breast.

If her encounter with breast cancer gave them anything, both Harshes say, it was perspective. They don't sweat even the not-so-small stuff.

Mrs. Harsh tells a story to illustrate:

A few months ago, Mr. Harsh fell in the garage and broke a leg. Seeing him on the floor, she feared the worst. When he said it was his leg, Mrs. Harsh replied: "Oh, thank goodness. We can fix that."

When she had finished telling the story, she looked at her husband and smiled.

"We've been around the block and back, haven't we, Mr. Harsh?"

NATURE ARTIST HAS A PERSONAL PARADISE

June 24, 2007

The sign on the garage says "Nature Sanctuary," but it's hardly necessary.

The property cheeps, twitters and buzzes with life on a warm spring morning. Barn swallows swoop around an outbuilding, voles squeak in a meadow, and flies buzz near an exotic flower that smells like rotten meat.

Welcome to Julie Zickefoose's 80 acres of rough-hewn paradise near Marietta.

She's an author, artist and radio commentator. Thanks to her nature essays on National Public Radio's *All Things Considered,* listeners all over the country have a mental image of what Indigo Hill, her homestead, looks like.

In person, it looks unpretentious, lush, a little shaggy. In other words, it's perfect for a woman who finds her bliss painting bluebirds and examining owl droppings.

"If I didn't have to go out for groceries, I would never leave," she said.

The house that Zickefoose shares with her husband, Bill Thompson III, and their two children lies off a country road in Washington County, about 125 miles southeast of Columbus.

A quarter-mile gravel drive winds through woods and meadows until a last turn reveals the house.

Chet Baker, the family's ultrafriendly Boston terrier, greets visitors by jumping into their cars.

Just outside the front door, bonsai trees that Zickefoose, 48, has been carting around since college rest on a shelf.

Below lies an exotic flower (*Sauromatum venosum*) that smells so strongly like something died, it draws flies. She just wanted to see whether she could grow one.

The house vaguely resembles a postmodern church: There's the main building and then off to one side, an art studio capped by a 42-foot-tall bird-watching tower that ends not in a steeple but a small observation platform.

Zickefoose climbs up there often to survey the property and tally bird species. (At last count, she was up to 183, including the indigo bunting, from which the property takes its name.)

"You can see things from up here and hear things that you wouldn't otherwise," she said. "Mostly I come up here to feel separate. It's like being on a boat."

A "dinner hook" hangs from the tower's lip in case she feels a need for refreshments. "You're four full flights of stairs up and you want a glass of wine. It's kind of an external dumbwaiter."

The property is exhaustively described in her 2006 book, *Letters From Eden: A Year at Home, in the Woods,* which contains essays and drawings of the creatures that roam her land.

That includes the venomous copperhead that bit her on the index finger as she was weeding under a shrub one summer.

She drove herself 18 miles to a hospital in Marietta, keeping her hand elevated the whole way. (People thought she was waving and waved back.)

The bite proved minor.

Zickefoose has been an avid bird-watcher since age 8, when she saw a blue-winged warbler taking a bath in a field behind her house in a suburb of Richmond, Va.

"That's a good age to set the hook. That's when many kids pick their life's passion."

She studied biology and art at Harvard, where she was known as Roller Girl for her habit of skating around campus.

After college she worked for the Nature Conservancy before establishing a career as a freelance artist whose illustrations have appeared in *The New Yorker, Smithsonian* and many other publications.

She met Thompson, whose family publishes *Bird Watcher's Digest* in Marietta, after he hired her to do a cover illustration for the magazine.

They scoured the Appalachian foothills for a place to live close to nature, and found Indigo Hill in 1992.

"It had to be secluded," Zickefoose said. She paused to take in the vista from atop her tower. "I wouldn't change a thing."

Her *All Things Considered* career began with an e-mail from anchorwoman Melissa Block, who was a college classmate. She has been delivering commentaries on the show since 2004.

Her most popular was about the bullfrog she put in her backyard pond, only to discover, to her horror, that it had developed a taste for hummingbirds. (The frog left tail feathers behind as evidence.)

She's also managed to incite a little controversy. In some cross talk with Block in April, she revealed that she "controls" sparrows that invade her bluebird boxes. (Kills them, in other words.)

"It was out of my mouth and then I thought, 'Oh boy.' So I was getting death threats by e-mail. People who said they hoped someone came and eliminated me. Over a house sparrow."

Ironically, Zickefoose is known all over Washington County as the person to call if you find an injured bird.

She has taken in many, and her book is full of episodes in which she stops to rescue a creature in distress.

Using both her science and art backgrounds, she finds wonder in scenes that most people would pass by without a second thought, said Jim McCormac, avian education specialist with the Ohio Division of Wildlife.

"She writes a lot about her property there, and, you know, she would admit this: It's not out of the ordinary but, like any land, it's filled with interesting things.

"She has a wonderful gift of pulling them out of the woods and presenting those animals and plants in ways that people would really want to know about them."

In her book, she writes about coming upon a dead opossum on one of her regular circumnavigations of the property.

She sifts the evidence—bird pellets, a partially eaten carcass—and concludes it was the work of a great horned owl.

"I realize I am laughing and talking to myself, and I have to laugh again at the thought of a woman moved to rapture by half a possum and two owl droppings."

FOR COUPLE, WEDDING BLISS EXTENDS 75 YEARS

June 19, 2008

Robert and Agnes Head were watching *The Price Is Right* on stacked televisions when I visited them recently.

He sat close to the top television, which is outfitted with a magnifying screen to accommodate his impaired vision.

She sat a few feet behind him and watched the bottom television, with the sound turned up to accommodate her faded hearing.

Making space for each other is nothing new to the Heads: They celebrated their 75th wedding anniversary this month.

They related their history in the manner of many a long-married couple: He would tell his version, then she would offer corrections.

"I want you to know my wife was No. 1 in her high-school class in studies," he said.

"No, I wasn't," she countered.

This much was undisputed: They have known each other since they started first grade in Greenfield (about 55 miles southwest of Columbus). And it was not love at first, second or third sight.

"I never paid any attention to him," Mrs. Head said. "He just lived about a block and a half down the street. To me, he probably was just a smarty little boy."

Things finally took off in high school, when Robert, a football and basketball player, began giving Agnes, the daughter of a grocer, generous portions when she came into the ice-cream shop where he worked.

"We started going together, and it just got to be a habit, I guess," Mr. Head said.

The habit proved impossible to break: They were married June 1, 1933, and have a son and a daughter, who are both in their 70s. In a marriage that began during the Franklin Roosevelt administration, they have endured a single separation: He was drafted into the Navy for two years during World War II.

When he left for Cincinnati in a car with other inductees, she cried secretly so as not to burden him with her tears. He felt like crying but didn't.

"I had some other boys with me," he explained.

Mr. Head, who retired from Dayton Power & Light, is stooped, uses a walker and is recovering from a fall that broke a bone in his neck. But he's good-natured, given to punctuating his sentences with an agreeable "yeah."

Mrs. Head scolds him for not wearing his dentures, but she also caters to him by driving to McDonald's for fish sandwiches.

"See, without his teeth, he has problems. But he can eat a fish sandwich."

If it's raining, however, no fish.

"I don't drive in the rain," she said.

They spend most of their time in the back room of the white frame house where they have lived since after World War II. It's outfitted for comfort: the televisions, several recliners, photos of grandchildren and great-grandchildren and a needlepoint rendering of the 23rd Psalm.

They like watching Cincinnati Reds games together. He tells her what the commentators are saying, and she tells him what the camera is showing.

As they posed for a photo, Mrs. Head rested a hand on Mr. Head's leg and smoothed a wrinkle in his shirt. She calls him Heady. He calls her Lil (her middle name is Lillian).

Mr. Head said he didn't buy his wife anything for their 75th anniversary. Mrs. Head—sitting with her mate of three-quarters of a century—said she didn't mind: She already has everything she needs.

HE'S THE MASTER OF GOURDIAN KNOTS

Aug. 21, 2008

This is the time of year when Roger Kline ties gourds in knots.

It's a delicate operation.

"You got to have 90-degree temperatures," he said. "The gourd's got to be limber. It's got to be about 5 o'clock in the afternoon."

As he said this, it was about 9:30 in the morning and temperatures were in the 80s. But Kline was willing to risk it for the benefit of the media.

"All right, all right. We're going to try it," he said, gently grasping a tender young gourd between meaty fingers.

"You ready? Just the oil on your hands when you touch them could kill them. Everything shocks them. . . . Oh, oh, oh. There!"

If gourd-suspense movies existed, he could write scripts for them.

Kline, 65, has a farm and a roadside produce market on 40 acres on Rt. 104 in Ross County. The corn, tomatoes, peppers and melons that he grows await hungry passers-by. A hand-lettered sign invites them to leave their money in a rusty tin can.

The farm is the family homestead, established in 1923 by Kline's grandfather. Kline was born just up the road in Yellowbud, named for the yellow wildflowers that grew on the banks of the Ohio-Erie Canal that cut through it.

Kline, who lives alone, has been growing and selling pumpkins (his 414-pounder took top honors at the Circleville Pumpkin Show in 1982) since he was a boy.

About 15 years ago, he got into gourds, which possess the same magic: They make people want to spend money.

"I had a woman come in here from McArthur and spend $81 the other day. She's got a little shop."

A run-of-the-mill dried gourd might yield $2 or $3. But tie one that grows into a knot, and suddenly you're talking real money.

"I sell them for $25 to $50," he said. "You break them—that's why they're so high. I'll break one out of five."

Three years ago, Kline saw two dewy young gourds growing side by side and decided to try knotting one around the other.

"I was just lucky everything went right with it. Never done it again."

He considers it his masterpiece.

He wouldn't sell his double-knotted gourds for any amount. But if someone were to offer some anyway, he said, the price would be $500.

Those hoping for lucrative gourd commerce in October must be vigilant in August, when the variety known as "extra-long handle dippers" present their pliable little selves for knotting.

They're knotted at 2 days old, before they harden. Sometimes, they rot from being handled. If all goes well, though, they grow, and the knot descends until you have something resembling a strangulated baseball bat.

They're a novelty, but the real entertainment might lie in Kline's enthusiastic narration of the process.

"See, now, here's the secret," he said as he bent a pinky-sized gourd into a loop. "You just push it so far. You try to push it on through (the loop), and it'll snap every time. Take it real, real slow. . . . Oh, oh, I'm getting there—just a little more, just a little more. I got it!"

Babies have been born with less-breathless comment.

On the other hand, these are Kline's babies.

COBBLER HANGS ON AS CITY CENTER TUMBLES

Dec. 10, 2009

Shoe repairmen are stubborn, Dave Staley told me.

He was working on a stiletto heel recently when I stopped by his shop in the corridor that once led from the Hyatt on Capitol Square to City Center mall.

While Staley resoles shoes, the mall is literally crumbling a few feet away. Some days, he can hear the rumble of demolition over the whir of his sanders and polishers.

Yes, he acknowledged, business is down significantly. But Staley has a leathery determination: scuffed by hard times, but durable.

So he stays.

"I love the Downtown area," he said. "I love my customers, and I really would hate to leave, because at 47 years old, it would be like starting over."

Despite the mall's demise, the corridor containing the Shops on Capitol Square still has commerce: two restaurants, a florist, a dentist's office, a newsstand, and Staley Shoe Repair.

This year has been the roughest for him, Staley said. The mall closed in March, and, shortly thereafter, he was forced to lay off his lone employee, Tyrone Smith, 50. Smith had been shining shoes there for 13 years.

"The day I had to let him go, it was the hardest thing I had to do. It just pains me to think about it. I say a prayer for him every day before I go to bed."

Smith, who is still looking for a job, said he and Staley remain friends. Both cried the day he left.

"I don't blame him," Smith said. "Not one bit."

Staley, a Columbus native who was born with limited sight in one eye, has always liked working with his hands. He installed carpet for years before the wear and tear on his knees got to be too much.

In 1992, he bought the shoe-repair shop from another owner. City Center was 3 years old and bustling with pedestrian traffic.

"It used to be nonstop through this hallway."

Everyone knows the story from there: competing suburban malls were built, and City Center began its slide toward oblivion.

Loyal customers, though, have kept Staley going.

Pat McCune, the only visitor between about 3 and 4 p.m. on a recent weekday, stopped by just to say hello. McCune, who works Downtown, said he's been taking shoes to Staley for 14 years.

"He keeps my shoes going longer and wearing better than any place I've taken them," McCune said.

By virtue of his proximity to the Ohio Theatre and the Statehouse, Staley draws some unlikely customers. He has worked on shoes for entertainers Patty LuPone, Gregory Hines and Robert Duvall, as well as many politicians. When *The Lion King* came to town, Staley was called on to stitch up a lion's paw footwear. He's been asked to repair saddles, baseball gloves and car bras. And an exotic dancer once brought in some leather riding crops. "I didn't ask," Staley said. "I just fixed."

As his day wound down, the quiet in the hallway outside was broken only occasionally by the click of passing heels. Still, Staley was saying that he foresees the day when redevelopment of the mall site, and the city's push for Downtown living, will yield more customers.

Meanwhile, he said, he takes comfort in knowing that he does a job that can't be automated, outsourced overseas or eliminated. "The last time I checked, people still had to wear shoes."

NO ONE STORMS THE CASTLE WITHOUT HER PERMISSION

Dec. 31, 2009

"Bill told me I never have to turn in my security badge," Elaine Miseta said with a hint of pride.

After all, if you can't be trusted after 67 years at a company, at what point can you be trusted?

Miseta officially retired yesterday—on her 88th birthday—from her job as an administrative assistant at the White Castle corporate headquarters. Her first day was June 8, 1942.

The Bill who let her keep her security badge is Bill Ingram, president and chief executive officer. She also served his father, Edgar, and his grandfather E. W. "Billy" Ingram, founder of the restaurant chain famous for its little hamburgers.

Miseta was at the company eight years before the latest president was born. They've always been on a first-name basis, given that he was a toddler when they met.

"It's great to have someone who has that historic knowledge," said Ingram, 59. "She's very organized and methodical, and remembers everything."

Miseta—who was born near Montpelier, a village in the northwest corner of the state—moved to Columbus to take a job that her father helped her get with what was then called the Ohio Bureau of Unemployment.

She hated it.

"So I transferred to the highway department," she said, "and that was just as bad."

Miseta found her place when she walked into the White Castle headquarters, 555 W. Goodale St., to drop off an application and found it buzzing with activity.

"I thought, 'This is for me.'"

She started in the stenographer's pool but wound up serving as the executive secretary to the company leaders.

Until recently, callers had to get past her to reach Ingram.

"They want to talk to Mr. Ingram," she said. "Everybody does. If they have a hangnail, they want to talk to Mr. Ingram. But he doesn't do hangnails."

Miseta had a routine: She would arise at 5 a.m., dress in a suit (don't get her started on "business casual") and be in the office by 6:15. By the time the phones started ringing about 9 a.m., she had accomplished a lot. She would leave for home in Upper Arlington about 4 p.m.

When told that was more than eight hours, she shrugged.

"They got their money's worth."

Miseta was married for 54 years to husband Frank, a lawyer who died in 2004.

They traveled the world together. ("We've never been to Borneo and the two Arctics, but we've been everywhere else.") The couple had no children—one reason that Miseta kept working so long.

Her last day on the job was actually Dec. 4; she has been using up vacation time since then.

She had calls to screen, mementos to pack and goodbyes to say. She didn't cry.

"My mother tried to teach me not to be a bawl baby," she said. "So you just grit your teeth."

Retirement hasn't diminished her loyalty.

She still professes a fondness for her longtime employer's signature product: the Slyder.

But she admitted she hasn't recently bought a sack full of the little burgers with the big digestive effect.

"I don't eat them very often because I have to be careful," she said. "They're kind of high-powered."

WHEN ANGEL PERFORMS, HE WINGS IT

Feb. 25, 2010

Angel, the umbrella cockatoo, nibbled on my coat but chose not to throw up in my presence.

Oh, well, maybe next time.

Cockatoos (a type of parrot) regurgitate when they're feeling affectionate and want to feed you.

"It's a sign of love," explained the effervescent Diane Rush.

I went to see her because I had read that she and Angel are making their umpteenth annual appearance at the Mid-American Exotic Bird Society bird fair on Sunday.

Exotic doesn't begin to describe Angel. He eats peanut butter-and-jelly sandwiches, hits on blondes and tells his owners when to go to bed.

"If he decides it's time to go to bed, the king of England could be sitting in here, and he'd say, 'Night night,'" said Rush, a 75-year-old grandmother who lives in Westerville with her husband, Chuck.

She and Angel have been together 18 years, during which time she has taught him to ride a little bicycle, dunk a miniature basketball and—this is big—lie on his back and roll over.

"That's trust because the only time a bird lays on his back is when he's going to bird heaven."

Angel's somersaults wowed 'em when Rush and Angel appeared in 2003 on the *Late Show With David Letterman.* It was the bird's biggest foray into show business.

He has since gone back to playing nursing homes, libraries, clubs and pet exhibits.

Rush, slowed by back trouble, isn't an aggressive promoter. She has no agent and a somewhat informal pricing structure (a club once paid her in birdseed).

Angel was a featherless, pink 5-week-old when Rush, a retired occupational-therapy assistant, first saw him at the home of a breeder. He all but insisted she adopt him.

"He was just all over me. Talking, rubbing up against me. Just like, 'You gotta take me.'"

Rush soon realized she had bought herself a performer. She built him a little scooter and a miniature basketball hoop. She bought him the birdie cycle. Training took a lot of patience and thousands of sunflower seeds, his preferred reward.

Angel also likes peanut butter-and-jelly sandwiches, although he discards the bread.

He's a constant source of surprise. He remembers people (he greeted a veterinarian he hadn't seen in seven years with celebratory regurgitation) and has a discerning eye (although he might say "hi" to dark-haired women, blondes get an appreciative "Well, hello.")

If frightened, he can nip with painful results, one reason I didn't interfere when he tasted my coat.

All in all, I was impressed, but Rush runs into the occasional animal-rights advocate who isn't. One confronted her at a show and said, "How dare you make that bird perform?"

Rush had a ready answer: "I said, 'Ma'am, you don't make a parrot do anything. Not if you want to have a hand left.'"

MIKE HARDEN HAD A WAY WITH WORDS

Oct. 27, 2010

I've never known anyone who could do more with 500 words than Mike Harden.

Long before I became a columnist myself, I would read his work to answer the question "How did he do that?"

How did he make me feel as if I were there with him as he interviewed inmates on their way to jail at Christmas? How did he manage to bring subjects to life so expertly?

The obituary I wrote for Thursday's paper (Mike died Wednesday of cancer) mentioned that he loved to share what he knew about writing. I didn't have room to get specific.

But I do now. So, as a tribute, I'd like to pass on some of his writing advice. I think he'd be pleased.

He offered several tips to aspiring writers in a 1988 column. My favorite is this: "Never use a word in a story that you wouldn't use in a love letter."

In other words, write the way people talk. They say rain, not precipitation. They walk into buildings, not facilities. And I've never heard two people in normal conversation use the word gubernatorial.

Of course, in the interests of conveying information economically, journalists often have to resort to the stilted language of the news business. But you don't.

Mike also advised writers to learn as much about the physical world as possible.

"Sycamore is a much lovelier word than tree," he wrote.

He used that advice to take his readers places. The beach at a faded New Jersey resort had "patchy goatees of sea grass." His grandson was born on the night of a "bone-china moon radiant with a halo of haze."

The physical world includes man-made objects, by the way.

Mike knew that, if you want to give a sense of what it's like to be an Amish author, you'd better include the fact that the man in question cranked out his essays on "a Smith Corona word processor hooked to a 12-volt car battery."

He also advised young writers that their notes should include as many observations as quotes.

"What is in the bookcase behind your subject is sometimes as revealing as what he is saying."

When Mike rode in a sheriff's van with men who were going to spend Christmas in prison, he told us some of what they said and a lot of what they saw on a frigid December day.

"Through one-way windows latticed with bars, the riders drank in the passing vista—the light froth of snow on winter-shorn fields, the bluestem and ironweed hugging the guardrail along I-71.

"A few men, wearing nothing on their shoulders but the short-sleeved shirts they were arrested in last summer, stared blankly at Christmas lights and crèche kitsch set out for the season."

I'm pretty sure that says "bleak" better than anything those poor guys uttered.

By the way, who thinks of riding with prisoners at Christmas? A writer who knows that the best stories often lie in the gritty places where others would rather not look.

A writer like Mike Harden.

SHELTER SUPERVISOR HAD HER OWN TROUBLES

Nov. 23, 2010

Dianne Solomon walks fast, talks loudly and laughs easily, except when she reflects on where she was seven years ago.

Then she cries.

She works at the YWCA Family Center, an East Side homeless shelter that, like all other homeless shelters in Columbus, is overflowing with clients.

On a recent morning, families filled all 50 of the small rooms, and 19 others were in "overflow" at a Reynoldsburg hotel.

Solomon, 47, is the family-support lead supervisor, a position with a variety of duties—not the least of which involves waking everyone at 6:30 a.m.

"Good morning, families," she trills as she walks down the halls. "Good morrrning. Wakey wakey; rise and shine." (The children call her Wakey Wakey.)

Everyone wants something from Solomon: bus passes, tampons, the weather forecast, justice.

"Baby, listen to me; hear me out," she tells a young mother who thinks another resident damaged her cell phone. "Before we go accusing somebody, let's call Boost Mobile, see if there's trouble on your line."

Another mom approaches.

"You OK, hon? You look like you've been crying."

The mom's 3-year-old has been throwing up.

Solomon commiserates and assures her that she can stay behind with the child when the rest of the families, by rule, vacate the center at 8:30.

The 8:30 cutoff ensures that parents get their youngsters to school and themselves to job interviews, counseling or other pursuits meant to lift them from their situations.

Anyone who complains gets the Dianne Solomon story.

She was a crack addict with a baby girl seven years ago, before the new family center—at 900 Harvey Court—was built. Homeless families were bused to church basements to sleep, then awakened at 5 a.m. to be bused to the old Franklinton center, which offered services such as child care and job counseling.

"In here, it's a whole different story," Solomon said. "They have their own rooms. So when I hear a person complain, I'm like 'Come here. Let me tell you what used to be.'"

Every time she tells the story, tears well in her eyes.

Solomon got off drugs and, five years ago, was hired by the center when it opened. It's designed to shelter families for up to three weeks.

The center has child care, showers, a playground, a laundry, a dining room and a job-placement office. And it has been experiencing an overflow clientele since at least July.

So Solomon is always moving.

She defuses a domestic argument. She finds a winter coat for a woman. She admonishes a teenager to pull up his pants (the center has a rule against low-riding trousers). She steps into a storage room and frets about whether the center will have enough toys for all the children on Christmas.

As she bustles through the dining room, a little boy in a coat three sizes too big stops her.

"We're going to get a new house," the child says.

Solomon's eyes glisten again.

"Basically, that's the paycheck," she said: "when you see them housed."

BIG TOP BECKONS KING OF CALLIOPE

May 6, 2012

The Calliope King of the World lives in Gahanna. Who knew?

He's Myron Duffield, a jovial 79-year-old with a passion for playing tunes on unusual instruments. You should hear him on the musical skillets.

On Thursday, the king will enter a prized calliope realm: the circus.

When the Ringling Bros. and Barnum & Bailey Circus comes to town, Duffield will perform on the instrument for 20 minutes at the "pre-show" (a warm-up event preceding the main performance).

"I was a little bit shocked," Duffield said.

Calliopes, high-pitched keyboard instruments that force air through tuned whistles, were once fixtures at circuses and on riverboats. Myron fell in love with their happy sound in his boyhood home of Middleport on the Ohio River.

Later in life, he built his own calliope, and for the past 40 years he has played it at thousands of parades, fairs and festivals.

His son, Jeff, of Westerville, decided it was high time for his dad to play at a circus, too. He contacted Feld Entertainment, producer of the Ringling Bros. circus, and asked whether Myron could appear. Feld passed him onto Irvin Public Relations, its representative in Columbus, and pretty soon the king had his gig.

The Calliope Queen of the World will be there, too.

She's June, his wife of 58 years. It's a love story that began in the seventh grade.

"I kissed her for the first time by the big oak tree in the schoolyard," he explained.

They married after Myron's military service. They had two children and moved frequently during his career in data communications. They were living in northern Ohio in the 1960s when Myron decided to build a calliope for a Cub Scout parade float.

He assembled it from organ pipes, whistles, a vacuum cleaner motor and a piano keyboard. The float won first place, but Duffield wasn't satisfied with the calliope.

"I said to my wife that I've got to have a real one."

He bought what he describes as a pile of old calliope parts from a mechanical music dealer in Troy, Ohio, and turned them into an authentic instrument. The dealer is the person who first jokingly dubbed Duffield "Calliope King of the World," a title he quickly adopted.

Then he researched circus vehicles and, using salvaged and homemade parts, built a red wagon with wood-spoke wheels to transport his prize.

The calliope made its debut at a Fourth of July parade in 1972 in Medina, Ohio. Since then, it's been all over the Midwest. The Duffields charge a fee, but the calliope business is no way to get rich, they say.

"We wore out five cars and seven transmissions," Myron said.

June, 78, did most of the driving until a couple of years ago, when Parkinson's disease forced her to stop. Their son does the driving now.

The Duffields moved to Gahanna from Coshocton about a year and a half ago. When he's not touring as the Calliope King, Myron is often found at schools or retirement centers as "Professor Myroni." He has an hourlong act in which he plays antique instruments, such as cowbells, medicine bottles, musical saws, rattles and skillets.

But the calliope seems to be his biggest musical joy.

"Very few of the present generation have ever heard the joyous, exciting music of a calliope," he says in a brochure.

The Calliope King aims to remedy that wherever he can.

RIDE HOME LED TO LOVE OF LIFETIME

June 12, 2012

I asked Evelyn and George Foeller, married seven decades, an obvious question: How did you two meet?

She turned to him and said, "Now, don't you start."

Mr. Foeller, 92, likes to say he picked her up on the street—true but demanding of further explanation.

He and his brother, who knew the young Evelyn, offered her and a friend a ride from N. High Street up the hill on E. North Broadway to her home near Calumet Street in Clintonville.

"Actually, I didn't like him at first," said Mrs. Foeller, 89. "But I learned to like him."

I guess so: They had their first date at the Valley Dale Ballroom in June 1940, when he was 19 and she was 16. Next Tuesday will be their 70th wedding anniversary.

Here's a touching thing they told me: In 1943, with World War II raging, he was put aboard a troop ship bound for the Pacific theater on the same day she went into labor with their first child. Neither told the other what was happening. He wasn't allowed to, and she didn't want to worry him.

A few hours after the ship departed, a telegram reached Mr. Foeller. It said: "Daddy, I arrived at 4:32 Thursday afternoon and weigh 8 lbs one ounce. Mommy and I both doing fine. Love, Susie." He put the telegram in his knapsack and carried it through the battles of Saipan, Tinian and Okinawa.

Mr. Foeller, a Navy medical corpsman assigned to the Marines, had four brothers, all of whom served during or just after the war. Mrs. Foeller's four brothers did likewise. They all made it home.

Susie had no idea who he was when he showed up in 1945 after two years overseas. But it didn't take her long to warm up.

In a family history that his son-in-law compiled, Mr. Foeller recalls a neighbor saying, "Boy, if I had a million dollars, I'd give it to anybody just to have a little girl come and greet me like that little girl greets her daddy when he comes home from work."

Mr. Foeller spent his working life as a pharmacist. He's a living link to Foeller's Drug Store, owned by his father and uncles, and reputed to be the birthplace of the banana split. Several cities claim that distinction.

The Columbus claim says Foeller's aunt dreamed up the dish in 1904 for a soda-fountain customer at the pharmacy, 567 N. High St.

The Foellers had six children: five girls and a boy who had cerebral palsy and died before his second birthday. They're up to 18 great-grandchildren, with more on the way.

They aren't big on giving marital advice to younger generations. Things are too different now, they said. But, pressed on the matter, they repeated the oft-mentioned rule of never going to bed angry with each other.

Did they follow that dictum?

"Yes," Mr. Foeller said impishly, "especially when I was away in the service."

This month, they returned to the site of their first date. The Valley Dale was hosting an event honoring World War II veterans, so the Foellers took the opportunity to see the old place again. They didn't dance, but being there was pretty amazing, Mrs. Foeller said.

"It's still standing, and so are we."

AUDITOR SHOWS ARDOR FOR PRECISION

Aug. 14, 2012

I asked Alan Mayberry how much he had saved Union County that day.

"Fourteen dollars and 74 cents," he said.

Mayberry is highly precise.

The 19-year-old has Asperger's syndrome, an autism spectrum disorder characterized by, among other tendencies, a focus on detail and a love of routine.

As it happens, such behaviors also make someone a good deputy county auditor.

"He seems to have a real eye for detail," county Auditor Andrea Weaver said. "He does seem to enjoy repetitive tasks, or they don't bother him. And he really likes to find mistakes. He really likes it when somebody from another department has processed an invoice for payment and he can find some inconsistency. It's become a daily thing now, when Alan leaves, to tell us how much he saved the county."

Mayberry, a Marysville High School graduate, studies accounting at Columbus State Community College.

He met Weaver through WorkNet, a Union County Board of Developmental Disabilities program that prepares clients for the work force. She interviewed Mayberry to help him sharpen his job-seeking skills.

A few weeks later, when Weaver actually had a job opening, she remembered him.

When he called Mayberry with the good news, said Michael Heifner of WorkNet, the new employee had a memorable reaction: "I got a job! I got a job! I got a job!"

Mayberry started on June 6 and works three days a week.

On his desk are baskets full of purchase orders, invoices and payment authorizations.

He makes sure that the numbers match. He also makes sure that anyone spending county money abides by the guidelines, such as the prohibition against liquor on expense accounts.

He recently ran across a room-service purchase for "Choc Sedux" and didn't rest until he had established that it stood for an innocent dessert.

Mayberry has had a job coach, Sarah VanVoorhis, with him during his break-in period. She has helped him learn how to temper his demand for accuracy so that he accepts, for example, the automatic rounding of small amounts.

He has also needed help with social skills.

Mayberry, whose speech is halting at times, is opinionated about certain subjects and honest to a fault. If something strikes him as odd, he is apt to say so.

"Alan can't lie," Heifner said. "He's going to tell it like it is. No matter what it is, he's going to tell it like it is."

Weaver sometimes has to tell Mayberry when enough is enough.

"There have been moments," she said.

Mayberry hopes to complete an associate degree in a year or two and work full time as an accountant or auditor.

In the meantime, he probably qualifies as the most content Union County employee.

Besides reporting every day how much he saved the county, he also likes to repeat this sentence: "I love my job, and I love my life."

HANDMADE GUITARS STRIKE EMOTIONAL CHORD

Dec. 27, 2012

In the end, neither a numbed hand nor an aching heart could keep Howard Conkel from completing his Christmas gifts.

Last week, when I entered his house near Hilliard, I saw five guitars lined up in front of a fireplace—each tied with a ribbon.

Conkel, 66, made them for his five grandchildren: Kaylee, Kaity, Isaac, Olivia and Luke.

He calls the gifts "encouragement." He wants his grandchildren to grow up to find the same joy and solace in music that he feels.

Conkel plays the guitar himself, although he says he doesn't play it as well as he once did.

An avid woodworker, he was "fiddling around" on his table saw one day in 2004 when, in a moment of inattention, he let his left hand get too close to the blade.

The resulting wounds took 100 stitches to close and left him with three numb, unruly fingers. He fashioned a homemade hand brace to keep them in line.

"He went through a very troubled depression time," said Billie, his wife of 45 years. "But, thank the Lord, a wonderful surgeon did three major surgeries . . . and got his hand back to working."

Conkel demonstrated by accompanying himself on the guitar while singing—in a clear, strong voice—"Close to Christmas," a song he wrote.

He uses sight, not touch, to ensure that his numbed fingers have found the correct positions on the fret board.

Conkel, the son of a bridge builder who taught him how to handle tools, spent his childhood on the West Side.

While home on leave from the Army in 1967, he met Billie—who had just moved to Columbus from Kentucky—at the old Green Gables drive-in restaurant.

They were married three months later and eventually had two daughters, Becci and April, and a son, Aaron.

The idea for the guitar gifts hit him in 2008.

Aaron, a construction worker with two daughters (Kaylee and Olivia), loved the idea and began pursuing it with his dad. They used mahogany and a pattern from the Martin guitar company.

That summer, though, Aaron, 31, developed a drug-resistant infection on the back of his head. He fought it for three months, then contracted the flu.

"He went to bed, and the next morning I found him gone," his mother said.

His father lost interest in the guitar project. He still took comfort in music, but he found the thought of building the guitars without his son too painful.

This year, he retired from Columbus Showcase after 46 years and decided that the time had come to return to the effort.

The result: five guitars lovingly cut, sanded, lacquered and polished.

His grandchildren, ages 8 to 15, received the instruments with delight.

"Amazing," said Kaity Catalfina, 14. "I call my guitar my baby."

When she plays it, whatever the tune, she'll be telling the story of a grandfather's love and perseverance.

JOHN AND ANNIE GLENN CONTINUE JOURNEY TOGETHER

April 4, 2013

Annie Glenn held out her hand to show off the modest diamond ring that her husband, John, bought for $125—almost all the money he had in 1943.

He has offered many times to replace it with a bigger diamond.

She has always said no.

"It's shiny, and he picked it out," Mrs. Glenn said. "I don't need anything larger to make me happy."

On Saturday, they will celebrate their 70th wedding anniversary—another milestone in a marriage that has weathered two wars, 31 moves, two spaceflights and four Senate terms.

"I promised her on our wedding day I'd do everything I can to make sure our life is never dull," Mr. Glenn said.

The couple were sitting in his office at the John Glenn School of Public Affairs at Ohio State University, where he is chairman of the board of advisers.

"I'm not in here eight hours a day, five days a week or anything like that," said Mr. Glenn, who will turn 92 in July.

She is 93.

Both have had knees replaced, and she recently had cancerous cells removed from her nose. But, as Mr. Glenn puts it, they're still "kicking along pretty well."

The Glenns tell people they met in a playpen. Their parents, as young couples in New Concord, Ohio, were best friends who took their babies along when they visited.

They were both students at Muskingum College when Pearl Harbor was bombed. The conflict propelled Mr. Glenn into his career as a Marine fighter pilot who fought in both World War II and Korea.

The rest of his biography is well-known: supersonic test pilot, first American to orbit Earth, four-term senator from Ohio, oldest person on a space mission when he flew on the shuttle Discovery at age 77.

They've had lonely anniversaries and memorable ones. World War II and its aftermath kept the Glenns apart for about four of the first six years of their marriage. On their 16th anniversary, he learned he had been selected as an astronaut.

The Glenns, who have homes in Columbus and the Washington area, will celebrate their 70th with a quiet dinner on Saturday and, later this year, a trip to Norway with their two children and two grandchildren.

They're not gushy when they speak of their marriage, but flashes of emotion surface now and then.

He described how touched he was when he heard her speak fluently for the first time after speech therapy in her 50s largely freed her from a severe, lifelong stutter.

And she paused while explaining how their relationship helped them endure the cutthroat world of politics.

"John and I have always kept our closeness. . . . And it's been wonderful—just wonderful—because we had that real love. I'm going to cry, but it's true."

Neither has stopped looking ahead.

They have trips to take, birthdays to celebrate and an award to receive in May from the League of Women Voters.

"We're going to reach 100," Mrs. Glenn said, "and we're going to do it together."

HE FINDS PEACE IN BIRDS, BASEBALLS AND BREADBOXES

May 9, 2013

I asked Jim Van Buskirk how he would describe his eccentrically decorated mobile home.

"Hobo art," he said. "Hobo art is, you find things—or take things people give you. You pay nothing for it, and you do something with it."

Which explains the breadbox on the roof, the model ship hanging from the eves and the decorated oak door that is purely cosmetic.

Ohio Wesleyan University baseball players at nearby Littick Field occasionally hit foul balls into his yard. Van Buskirk incorporates them into his decor, too.

He is a thin 74-year-old, a retired antiques dealer, who finds a respite in art.

Hanging inside his house is a framed handwritten statement that he calls his philosophy. It says in part: "The things you see are a creation of mine, a gift from God, his way and my way of fighting depression. . . . If you think I'm different, well I am, and that is OK. We are all different."

Van Buskirk, one of nine children, was raised in orphanages and foster homes after his parents separated. His father had been disabled by a kick in the chest from a mule during World War II. His mother couldn't care for the children alone.

He was in high school when he met his future wife, Norma Jean. They wed the day before he left to serve a hitch in the Army. They were married for 37 years, had four children and ran Delaware antiques and appliance-repair businesses together. She died of kidney failure in 1994.

Depression hit him hard after a man murdered Van Buskirk's former daughter-in-law and 16-year-old granddaughter in 2004 in what

Morrow County authorities described as a domestic dispute. Two years later, he lost a son to cancer.

Van Buskirk, a cancer survivor himself, became so withdrawn and forgetful that doctors thought he had Alzheimer's disease.

Art proved to be better therapy than antidepressants, he said.

He paints in a small room next to the furnace in his narrow house.

"On the cold winter nights, I don't sleep much at night, so I turn the radio on and listen to the music and do my thing and let the winter pass."

He has an affinity for Pennsylvania Dutch hex signs and scenes inspired by the Little Brown Jug, Delaware's famous harness race.

He also loves birds. Two parakeets tweet in a floor-to-ceiling enclosure he built for them. Owl, cardinal, eagle and flamingo figurines dot the exterior. Wrens nest in the breadbox.

Van Buskirk said he has never heard a complaint about his unorthodox decor, but it does attract attention.

Wesleyan art students have photographed it. Occasionally, a passer-by asks for a tour.

When I asked, Van Buskirk was happy to oblige, walking the length of the exterior, explaining where he salvaged this sign or how he made that plywood cutout. Then we went inside, where he sat in his easy chair, looking content amid the photos, religious symbols, posters and paintings.

"I always wanted a little cabin in the woods," he said. "So I call this my little cabin in the city."

LIFELONG TEACHER EDUCATES ABOUT HER ALZHEIMER'S

May 14, 2013

Lou Willis spent her career as a teacher, and, at age 78, she continues to be one.

She offers instruction in how to live with Alzheimer's disease—because she has it.

Last week, she climbed the steps to a stage, took a deep breath and said: "I'm calling today my coming-out party. I'm openly admitting that I have Alzheimer's disease."

The scene was brave, touching and educational.

Lou, who wound up a long career in education when she retired as assistant principal at Barrington Elementary School in Upper Arlington, was told more than a year ago that she has the progressive brain disease that affects memory.

It afflicts more than 200,000 Ohioans.

I see Lou just about every Sunday at North Broadway United Methodist Church but didn't suspect that anything was wrong. She told me a couple of months ago after deciding that she could do more good by discussing it than hiding it.

Raising money to combat a disease isn't easy if everyone tries to keep it a secret.

Her first semi-public step occurred this year when she addressed social-work students at Ohio State University to help them understand the disease from a patient's point of view.

Afterward, she told her family she was thinking about becoming more public about her condition.

"You go, girl," said her daughter, Lynne Willis Steger.

Last week, she spoke to people gathered at the McConnell Arts Center of Worthington for an event by the central Ohio chapter of the Alzheimer's Association called "Celebrating Hope."

Because the title sounds optimistic for so terrible a disease, Lou was eager to correct any misimpressions.

Sure, she said, the diagnosis was a blow: After the doctor told her, she went home, retreated to her bedroom and cried.

"My first pity party," she said.

But then she decided she couldn't just surrender to it. So she continued with her life.

She still takes walks, still goes out with friends. She regularly attends meetings of a support group, organized by the Alzheimer's Association, for people in the early stages.

Lou handed out a list of a dozen pieces of advice. No. 1: "No matter what else, you have to live your life." No. 3: "Go someplace every day. Get out whenever you can." No. 10: "Forgive yourself for not remembering things."

The disease has taken some things from her already: Bill, her husband and caregiver, does the cooking. She had an assistant hold reminder cards while giving her speech to make sure she said all that she had planned. She no longer plays bridge.

And she knows how Alzheimer's disease ends.

In the meantime, she intends to stay active—even when it's difficult.

"Some days you have to be gutsy," she said. "Or, as we say at our house, some days you just have to suck it up."

PIGS BECOME CAMERA HOGS FOR TRAY OF CAKE MIX

July 30, 2013

Steve Mapes buys 100 boxes of cake mix at a time.

"People ask me if I'm making a wedding cake," he said. "I say, 'No, I'm feeding it to hogs.'"

Hogs love dry cake mix—Pillsbury Funfetti in particular.

That's the type of thing you learn after more than four decades of swine photography.

Mapes, 60, is the official swine photographer of the Ohio State Fair. It is his job to get an uncooperative species to cooperate.

"They're the hardest animals," Mapes said. "I've had boars attack me because they're all fired up and I smell like other boars."

But there is money in those ill-tempered beasts. The world-record auction price for a prize boar (a male used for breeding) is more than $200,000.

Exhibitors want photographs that emphasize their prize animals' potential to produce meaty offspring.

So the photos are shot in profile with the body stretched (to emphasize length), the legs staggered (to hint at body width) and—ideally—the head turned slightly away (to make the loin muscle that runs along the back stand out).

Of course, the pig isn't particularly interested in modeling. So Mapes poses the smiling exhibitor, then shouts directions to an off-camera "puller" who moves a tray of goodies back and forth to tease the pig into position.

"If you just let them just stand there and eat, they'll look like crap."

The best subjects arrive hungry, but pigs are so well-fed these days, they need to be enticed with something special, Mapes said.

Hence the Funfetti.

Given the difficulties, exhibitors seem to have no qualms about paying Mapes $25 for a 5-by-7-inch digital print.

He'll shoot 450 to 500 animals before the fair ends. And then he'll immediately head for the Indiana State Fair to do the same.

"He knows how to get animals to do what he wants," said Kayla Overstake of Hillsboro, an exhibitor who posed with her grand- and reserve-champion pigs.

"He's the premier photographer."

Mapes, who grew up raising pigs on a Union County farm, started photographing them shortly after high school, when he noticed that the only swine photographer he knew was getting old.

"I thought I could take over that business."

He travels from coast to coast almost year-round, photographing swine at fairs, livestock shows and other events.

Sometimes his son-in-law or grandsons help, but he's mostly a one-man operation.

He lives in Milford Center, in Union County, with his wife, Rebecca.

The couple's 43rd wedding anniversary was June 29, but they have yet to celebrate it, Mapes said.

"I was at a hog show in Illinois."

AMINAH ROBINSON AT 75

Feb. 15, 2015

Aminah Robinson's kitchen is all but filled by an exuberant sculpture that incorporates doors, coffee jars, sticks, clothespins and music boxes.

On a long table in her living room lies a colossal, scroll-like fabric piece on which she has worked since 1958.

Not even she knows how long it is.

A back room added in 2007 ("I promised I'd keep it clean," she says a little naughtily) is stuffed with countless works in progress and materials—shells, hooks, buttons, brushes—to create even more works.

The only creature moving easily through Robinson's modest East Side house is Baby, her tiny Chihuahua. Everyone else must proceed with caution because her home is dedicated to art, not ease of access.

Robinson, a MacArthur "genius grant" recipient whose work has been shown in several art museums, remains driven by an intense need to tell through art the story of her family, her community and her African-American heritage.

She is celebrating a landmark birthday—she's turning 75—with an exhibit at Hammond Harkins Galleries in Bexley.

"We're going to be showing some of her work that's never been seen," said Marlana Keynes, the gallery owner. "She's an absolute genius when it comes to expressing her life."

The artist, born Brenda Lynn Robinson, lived much of her childhood in Poindexter Village, then a new public-housing complex.

She has often told the story of not speaking until she was 5 or 6 years old. She doesn't know the cause of the speech deficit, but it taught her to express herself in other ways.

Her father, a janitor who at times worked four jobs, made her sketchbooks and encouraged her to express herself through drawing.

"He would say, 'Tell me, Bren, what do you see?' So I would take out my little notebook and begin to draw. And that was my only way of communicating."

Her father also introduced her as a child to Roman Johnson and Emerson Burkhart, two of Columbus' foremost artists of the 20th century. They would let her sketch alongside them when they set up easels in the street.

Later, she studied art at the Columbus College of Art & Design (then called Columbus Art School) and Ohio State University.

In the years that followed, she married, had a son, divorced and was briefly on welfare. Through it all, she continued to produce art.

In 1974, she became an art instructor for the Columbus Recreation and Parks Department, and slowly her reputation grew.

She began calling herself Aminah in 1980 after a trip to Africa during which a holy man gave her the name, which means faithful or trustworthy.

By 1990, she had earned enough respect to win a commission for one of her best-known public works: A staircase mural at the Main Library of the Columbus Metropolitan Library. (In storage during building renovations, the work on canvas will return in 2016). The $500,000 MacArthur award followed in 2004.

The word that comes up repeatedly in conversations with Robinson is community.

Her densely layered fabric books and the scroll-like works she calls RagGonNons (because they go on and on) are full of references to Poindexter Village, a predecessor neighborhood called Blackberry Patch and their connections to the African-American experience in general.

The house she has lived in since 1974 is about 2 miles from where Poindexter Village, now mostly demolished, stood. Neighbors and friends are constantly dropping off buttons, clothespins, bottles, neckties and other materials that Robinson incorporates into her art.

"A lot of the time they throw it over the gate, and so a lot of the work and the materials are from people I don't even know," she said. "But some of them, many of them, I do. . . . It's a collective of community."

She rises every morning at 4 a.m., has a sweet roll and coffee, and works in an area off the kitchen that she calls the "painted study room," where she paints whatever comes into her head. Often, it has something to do with her family, her ancestors or the neighborhoods that shaped her. She folds the studies over on themselves because the sensations they create are so intense.

"I have to cover stuff, because they all talk. . . . It's like a community coming to talk to you, a whole bunch of people."

Behind the kitchen and painted study room lies the 2007 addition, which she calls her sanctuary.

A worktable runs the length of one wall, holding hundreds of brushes. Stacked sketchbooks sit here and there. Another sculpture, similar to the one in the kitchen, fills one corner.

Her long fingers playing over a fabric book she has been working on, Robinson pats it gently and concedes the obvious: She has run out of room and yet can't stop creating.

Back in her living room, she carefully unfolds some of Themba, the RagGonNon she began in 1958 to tell the story of a great aunt who was born a slave. It has rivers of buttons, miles of stitching, acres of fabric.

Yet what looks exquisitely detailed to a visitor (the MacArthur Foundation called her work "Homeric" in scale) looks incomplete to her. She adds something to it every day because the community's story must be told.

Often, she sleeps on the couch next to it.

"This is the way I work," she says. "This is the way I live."

AFTER 70 YEARS, COUPLE STILL CLICKS

Sept. 1, 2015

On the dining-room table at the home of Al and Ethel Jungeberg near Lewis Center lay a photocopy of the type of letter that no one throws away.

Limited to what he could fit on a single piece of paper, Mr. Jungeberg didn't waste words.

"Dearest Ethel," he began: "To let you know that I'm still alive & all right."

The Jungebergs—he is 93; she is 89—are marking their 70th wedding anniversary today. Married on Sept. 1, 1945, at a church in Berea, Ohio, they went a few days later to Miami for a honeymoon that was punctuated by a hurricane. Compared with events before the wedding, they said, it seemed a mild inconvenience.

Alvin Jungeberg met Ethel Klinect at a church youth event when both were in high school.

"It didn't click right away," Mrs. Jungeberg said.

By the time he was drafted into the Army in 1942, it was definitely clicking.

Mr. Jungeberg, a staff sergeant, was captured by German soldiers during the Battle of the Bulge in December 1944. The Army informed family members in January 1945 that he was missing in action.

For weeks, they knew nothing of his fate. Then, on March 5, the letter to Ethel arrived.

"Please see that my mother and father are taking this the best they can," he wrote.

His parents had already lost one son in the war.

Mr. Jungeberg was liberated on April 29 from a prisoner-of-war camp in Germany. He arrived in the United States a month later, emaciated and suffering from hepatitis.

Not long afterward, he took Ethel to a park in Berea and asked her to marry him.

For the wedding, she wore a white satin gown with a long train; he wore his Army uniform. World War II ended the next day.

The Jungebergs lived most of their lives in the Cleveland area, where he worked as a printer for newspapers. They had two children: a son, Ken, who lives near Cincinnati; and a daughter, Kathy Ann, who died of breast cancer at age 22.

"You never get over it," Mr. Jungeberg said.

They are great-grandparents now. He has given up driving, and she is about to.

Until a few years ago, they still cut the grass themselves, with one mowing a strip while the other rested.

Mr. Jungeberg, whose diet as a POW consisted largely of bread made of potato flour and sawdust, has always been easy to cook for, his wife said: He'll eat anything.

He is known for his exhaustive knowledge of big-band lyrics. To demonstrate, he broke into a couple of verses of "I'll Be With You in Apple Blossom Time."

As he reached the part that goes, "What a wonderful wedding there will be," Mrs. Jungeberg gently reached up to straighten his glasses.

He continued: "What a wonderful day for you and me."

HOTEL GUESTS REGISTER HIS NAME, FACE, MANTRA

Nov. 29, 2015

He sings. He hugs. He bursts into business meetings with motivational messages.

At the Hampton Inn & Suites at 501 N. High St., Clifford Steward has the official title of bellman—but would someone call Taylor Swift merely a guitar player?

It doesn't begin to describe the influence.

"He's just a delight to be around," said guest Ron Rogers of Kenton, in town for a recent convention. "Everybody at the convention center was talking about him."

On a recent morning, Steward, 51, strolled through the hotel breakfast buffet—telling women they're beautiful and warning men that he was stealing their car keys so they couldn't leave.

He stopped to chat with Joe Kahl and Cherelle Hollis, visiting for an insurance-company sales meeting.

Steward, Kahl said, had inspired a colleague to change his PowerPoint presentation to include a signature Steward phrase: "Claim your day."

It means "Think positive," the bellman said. "You know: Make things happen. To me, it's a powerful phrase to help people not to doubt themselves."

Steward was a home aide for people with disabilities until he took the Hampton job 11 years ago. He has since established himself as the face of the hotel, which hosts plenty of people attending events at the Greater Columbus Convention Center across the street.

During recurring events, such as the Arnold Sports Festival, people who have met him in years past stop to say hello even when they aren't staying at the hotel. Often, he poses for pictures with them.

"He bleeds hospitality," Hampton manager Matt Kolbrich said.

Occasionally, Kolbrich said, he has to ask Steward to tone down the exuberance a little, lest he overwhelm a guest.

Recently, Steward was a couple of hours into his morning routine when a guest requested his presence at a meeting in a hotel conference room. The attendees needed a shot of energy, she said.

Steward entered to a round of applause and launched into a brief pep talk, highlighted by both "Claim your day" and his other signature phrase: "God love you."

He walked out to more applause, singing softly to himself—as he is prone to do.

The singing "keeps my spirit up as well as other people's," he explained—"'cause guess what? I need my spirit up, too."

Back in the lobby, he caught sight of a Florida couple, Doug and Tenia Wonch, who visit Columbus annually to install the dance floor for the Ohio Star Ball.

"Oh, my God," he exclaimed, hurrying across the lobby to embrace them in hugs.

"He goes all out," Mrs. Wonch said—"way out of his way."

FAIR CHANCE IS ALL THAT ACTS SEEK

Jan. 12, 2016

The 8-foot woman stood talking to a juggler in a sombrero—just outside a room with a one-man band, Abraham Lincoln and a guy with a monkey on his shoulder.

Yes, the Ohio Fair Managers Association was in town.

The people who run fairs throughout the state gathered during the weekend at the Greater Columbus Convention Center for seminars, social events and a trade show featuring an eclectic assortment of acts vying to be hired.

If the trade show were a public event, it would be a way to sample a year's worth of county-fair entertainment in an afternoon. In just one circuit around one exhibit room, I talked to:

- Jeff Beal of Iowa, half of the Real Beals, a one-man-band act. He is the band, and wife Nancy, the singer.

  When they aren't operating a cleaning business, the Beals entertain at fairs and nursing homes.

  He prefers fairs.

  "We can do newer rock 'n' roll there," he said.

- Jesse Moore of Cleveland, who had a capuchin monkey on his shoulder.

  "These are the smartest of all monkeys," he said. "It's easy to train them. Well, I shouldn't say easy, but they're very trainable."

  While he talked, the monkey, Lincoln, furiously licked a red lollipop—his reward for shaking hands and giving hugs to passers-by on command.

Moore, of Sunshine MonkeyShines, is known as one of the last of the old-time organ grinders—although, at age 23, he isn't an old-timer himself.

- The Masked Blue Angel, a taciturn 16-year-old who preferred to let his manager, Bobby Fulton of North Carolina, discuss their wrestling act.

  Snapping into his wrestling persona, Fulton said that any fair manager who fails to hire Professional Bigtime Wrestling will face terrible retribution from the Masked Blue Angel.

While making my way out of that room, I passed a Lincoln impersonator, a Kiss tribute band and a man who had inserted himself into a 13-foot-tall tyrannosaurus costume.

In the hallway, I ran into the sombrero-wearing Steve Mills—billed as a "legendary performer from Marion."

His claim to fame is Mills' Mess, an offbeat juggling style he invented.

He demonstrated several juggling routines, unperturbed by the occasional drop.

People like to see jugglers drop things, he said.

He was chatting with Heather Mason of the Cincinnati Circus Co., who was towering over the crowd on stilts that made her more than 8 feet tall.

The challenging part about working at fairs is that so much happens at them, it's hard to stand out, she said.

You could say the same for the convention.

ROBBY MADE SUNDAY MORNINGS BRIGHT

April 21, 2016

As the end neared for Robby McDaniel, his family and friends eased his passage by singing his favorite song: "Tomorrow" from *Annie.*

Its upbeat lyrics suited the man, just 29 when he died last week. He had a way of making the sun come out.

His death leaves a void at North Broadway United Methodist Church, where I am a member. Robby, son of Ron and Becky McDaniel of Clintonville, was well-known for standing just inside the church entrance every Sunday and greeting people with unrivaled affection.

He told men they were handsome and women they were beautiful—or sometimes "prettyful." He dispensed hugs and handshakes. He said "Good morning" as if he meant it.

"He always said, 'That's my job,'" said his mother. "He found his niche."

Robby was born with Down syndrome. His parents said they always tried to accommodate his developmental disabilities without surrendering to them. Robby, the second-born of five children, played baseball, joined the Boy Scouts, graduated from high school and worked at ARC Industries.

"He was more like any other kid than not like them," Ron said.

Robby loved food, which made him easy to find in a pinch. Once, on a Boy Scout camp-out, he wandered away, and Ron found him seated with another troop, eating a hot dog. (The bun and ketchup were his favorite parts; he'd been known to stash an unwanted wiener in the couch cushions.)

Some children with Down syndrome are born with heart problems, but Robby, after surgery for a cleft palate in infancy, enjoyed good health.

But, on April 10, his body was suddenly overwhelmed by a fast-moving infection, possibly sepsis. He collapsed at home and was rushed to Ohio Health Riverside Methodist Hospital.

As he lay in a coma, no one knew whether he was aware of the people gathered around him. In case he was, though, they sang him "Tomorrow" and selections from *The Sound of Music*, his favorite movie.

"Mommy can't fix this," Becky told him in his final minutes. He died on April 12.

The church is remembering him with a computer slide show featuring photos and a series of short statements from his friends.

"Sweet Robby knew no strangers," said one.

"Who will tell me I'm 'prettyful'?" asked another.

After a funeral that celebrated all the things that Robby embodied, he was buried Saturday next to his grandparents in Forest, Ohio. His church name tag was pinned on his shirt.

On Sunday at North Broadway, a picture of Robby, looking jaunty in sunglasses, hung in memoriam, just above the spot where he always stood.

I was glad the sun shone brightly that morning, because we all needed to see it.

DR. SHINE ADDS GLEAM TO AIRPORT WINGTIPS

June 26, 2016

Dr. Shine stands in Concourse B, scouting for wingtips or penny loafers amid the passing parade of sandals and athletic shoes.

When he spots the right footwear, he beckons the owner.

"Sir, this is the best seat in the whole world right there," he says, motioning to his shoeshine stand. "This is the shoe clinic, the home office."

Summertime is slow in the shoeshine business, but Harry Batte—aka Dr. Shine—is familiar with the rhythms of his livelihood: He has been at it for almost 60 years, the past 12 at Port Columbus.

The recent terminal remodeling compelled him to relocate to a side hall leading to restrooms—a spot less visible than his old one in the concourse.

So the 74-year-old works hard to coax business his way.

In the hour I spent with him, he served four customers with an $8 shine for each.

A correlation seems to exist between flashy socks and shoeshine receptivity: Jack Denker of Georgia sported argyles; Michael Brickman of Dallas boasted multicolored stripes.

Both pronounced themselves pleased with the service, which includes crisp towel snapping and energetic brushing.

"My doctor said it's good for me," Batte said—"like aerobics."

More than 20 years ago, he suffered two heart attacks and a stroke, with the latter causing his lip to droop and an arm to weaken. But few people could tell now.

God healed him, said Batte, also an ordained minister.

"My lip straightened up; my arm straightened up. I started running because I was so happy."

He was just a child in Cincinnati when he first became fascinated by a shoeshine parlor in his neighborhood. His mother had to drag him out of the shop.

When he was 17, a shoeshine taskmaster took him under his wing.

"He was determined I was going to have those shoes looking like glass. If not, he would have me do it over and over and over again. And now I'm glad he taught me that way."

Batte had a stand at a Cincinnati hotel, where he shined many an athlete's shoe: Johnny Bench, Pete Rose and other members of the Cincinnati Reds plus a lot of visiting opponents.

He moved to Columbus in the 1980s when he remarried after his first wife died.

With a preacher's earnestness and a businessman's savvy, Batte likes to tell each customer that he—or, rarely, she—is the most important person in the world.

"The secret to a good shine is putting your whole heart into it. It's all about customer service."

ARENA HOLDS SAD MEMORY OF THE FATHER THEY LOVED

March 28, 2017

When you hear "St. John Arena," you might think of basketball glory.

When Melody Millar hears the name, she thinks of an auburn-haired ironworker who left for his job one Monday in 1955 and didn't return.

"He was a homebody," she said. "A family man. Just a good guy."

He was her dad, John Browning Jr.

Mementos linking Millar, 74, and her sister, Melanie Elfrink, 65, to their dad were laid out on a dining-room table when I visited them: a photo album, the folded flag presented at his funeral, his wallet, a metal hard hat with "John" stenciled across the front.

Millar was 12 and Elfrink 3 when their father, 36, slipped off a girder and fell 90 feet to his death while helping to build the arena.

Elfrink knows him only from what her family has said: that she worshipped her dad, racing to greet him when she heard his truck coming down the street.

"Mom said they didn't take me to the funeral home because I'd have climbed in (the casket) with him," she said.

The razing of St. John Arena, the home court of some great Ohio State basketball teams from 1956 to 1998, has been envisioned in Ohio State University's long-range plans for some time. Every time the sisters hear of it, they feel sad and sentimental.

"It's almost like if they tear that down, it's the last thing we had of him," Elfrink said.

"It's the end," Millar added.

Their father, a North High School graduate, met their mother, West High graduate Anna May Doelker, at a dance. They were married in 1941 at Parris Island, South Carolina, where Browning was in Marine training during World War II.

Knee injuries forced him out of the military, and he returned home to work as a house painter and an ironworker. He was also an amateur boxer and an avid outdoorsman.

After having two daughters, he wanted a son, and the wish came true when John Browning III was born in 1954. John Browning Jr. was thrilled. The family story is that on Jan. 9, 1955, a Sunday, he spent most of the day carrying 8-month-old Johnny around the house.

The next day, Browning's first on the job at the arena, he was killed.

Elfrink wants people to know about John Browning Jr. while the arena, named for the former athletic director Lynn St. John, still stands. When she hears "St. John Arena," it takes her back to childhood, when her young mind settled on the only explanation for the name that made sense.

"I thought they named it after him. Being a little kid, I thought, 'Wow, they named it after my dad.'"

IRISH TEENS TEAM UP TO PUZZLE OVER BASEBALL

July 30, 2006

There's so much to explain about an American baseball game: runs, hits, errors, Dippin' Dots, mascots and free bread.

Recently, I accompanied two teenagers from Northern Ireland to their first baseball experience, a Columbus Clippers doubleheader.

Bronagh Fox and Helen McMorris, both 16, were visiting as part of the Children's Friendship Project for Northern Ireland, a program that sends pairs of teens—one Protestant, one Roman Catholic—to the United States for month-long visits meant to build peace and understanding.

Bronagh and Helen seemed to understand each other well. Baseball, however, they found a little difficult to grasp.

At one point, a Clipper got caught in a rundown between second and third, and was tagged out. Then an umpire decided that the runner was safe because the pitcher had balked. Then all the umpires met and decided that, no, the runner was out after all. Then a coach ran onto the field to protest. Then the crowd booed lustily.

Rather than try to explain the scene, I told the teens to just think of it as akin to a U.N. deliberation: messy and frustrating but marginally better than chaos.

Bronagh and Helen, who left for home yesterday, stayed in Dublin with Mark and Teresa Dorow and their children, Ryan and Brittany.

Although the two teens are from the same county in Northern Ireland, they hadn't met until they signed up for the program. They didn't talk politics, at least to outsiders, but it lurks in the background: The aim of the program is to build bridges between two religious groups that have long been at violent odds in Northern Ireland.

Mr. and Mrs. Dorow themselves are an example of interreligious cooperation: He's Protestant; she's Catholic. That was one reason, Mr. Dorow said, they wanted to participate.

With the Dorows as hosts, the young visitors had a full plate of American experiences: They visited Washington (the Smithsonian's National Air and Space Museum wowed them); saw fireflies for the first time; and learned to love exotic fare such as waffles, graham crackers and sloppy joes (Helen affectionately calls them "burgers gone wrong").

Bronagh and Helen both said they had imagined the United States as a nation of skyscrapers and freeways, so the leafy suburbs and broad farmland of central Ohio surprised them.

Their initial response to baseball was a detached politeness. When a Clipper hit a line drive into the gap in left field and raised a dust cloud diving into third base, Helen's comment was, "Well, so much for the white uniform."

Later, a Clipper executed a sacrifice bunt. Mr. Dorow explained that the batter purposely made an out so the runner on first could advance to second. To which Bronagh replied, "That was nice of him."

After several innings, though, the teens had figured out what stirs American fans.

"Everybody goes mad for the long ball," Helen observed.

"I want to see that," Bronagh said and, to demonstrate her fan loyalty, added, "for us."

They also sampled Dippin' Dots ("very nice," Bronagh said), watched mascots LouSeal and Krash dance to "Y.M.C.A." on a dugout roof and noticed that baseball seems as much about eating as playing (aside from the concession delights, it happened to be bread-giveaway night—every fan leaving the stadium got a loaf).

In short, baseball did nothing to lessen Bronagh's evaluation of her American experience.

"Most things," she said, "exceeded my expectations."

FLAG REPRESENTS PRICE PAID BY MIA/POW FAMILIES

Jan. 6, 2011

On Monday afternoon, Sandra Paul was waiting for a special visitor in her Clintonville home.

The occasion demanded that she once again recount details of an event that consumed her life: On Dec. 20, 1972, her son Craig, a 26-year-old electronic warfare officer in the Air Force, was aboard a B-52 bomber that was shot down over North Vietnam.

Paul is a cheerful, energetic woman who calls herself the Candy Lady for her habit of handing out treats far and wide. But when the subject turns to Craig, a 1964 graduate of Whetstone High School, she speaks with surprising frankness.

"They (the North Vietnamese) said that he was killed in the plane crash, but that wasn't true. In 1977, when we got his remains back—of course it was the skeleton, you understand—there was a bullet hole in his forehead."

She thinks he survived the crash but was interrogated and executed.

During the five years between the crash and the return of her son's remains, Paul became a force to be reckoned with. She quit her teaching job and became Ohio coordinator of what is now called the National League of POW/MIA Families.

Before he died in 1996, her husband, Ken, told her he doubted that Craig's remains would ever have come home had she not been so persistent.

Today, she lives on a smaller teacher's pension but a much fuller heart for having been able to bury her son. The POW-MIA flag still flies beneath the American flag in her front yard.

"24/7," she said, careful to add that she lights the flagpole, as protocol requires, for nighttime display.

The flags are there so people won't forget, but people do forget. Hence, Paul's visitor this week: Thomas Mitchell, Ohio chapter director of Honor and Remember, a nonprofit organization with a goal of bestowing a special flag on families that have lost loved ones in war.

The group is pushing to have the flag, featuring a gold star against a field of red, officially recognized by Congress, said Mitchell, of Hamilton.

When Paul heard about the effort last year, she called Mitchell and told him she wanted to donate to the cause. Then she told Mitchell her story, and he immediately put her high on the list of people who should receive flags.

Paul's husband, whom she married in 1943, was a waist gunner on a B-17 bomber that flew missions over Germany during World War II. They were married for 53 years. After his death, she flew on a restored B-17, just to feel a little of what he felt.

("I got a little weepy," she said.)

Her younger son, Steven, who lives in Pickerington, served in the Navy during Vietnam and returned home safely.

And Craig is buried at the Air Force Academy in Colorado, the place he was wed two years before his death.

Mitchell, who himself has two sons serving in Afghanistan, presented the flag with minimal ceremony.

For a mother still missing her son, the banner—3 by 5 feet and bearing the name of Craig Paul—said all that needed to be said.

UNSCIENTIFIC OBSERVATIONS

YOUR BRAIN ISN'T READY TO ORGANIZE EVERYTHING

Jan. 12, 2017

Welcome to Joe's organizing tips for 2017.

I take an unconventional approach to the subject based on my belief that humans have not yet evolved the ability to keep track of the thousands of objects found in the average American household.

It took our species thousands of years to learn how to arrange sticks and leaves into a passable shelter. You can't expect us to hit on a way to keep our computer cords untangled and Legos sorted in just a few decades.

So either limit yourself to a spear and a loincloth, as our ancient forebears did in their primitive huts, or accept the fact that our brains lack the capacity to deal with an overload of stuff.

Still determined to try? OK, I will offer some organizing ideas, but remember what I said about unconventional.

Let's begin with receipts. Throw them away. I mean all of them: receipts for charitable contributions, state and local tax payments, stock purchases, whatever.

Then dare the IRS to audit you. It probably won't. But if it does, you'll end up in prison, where rules will prohibit the possession of all but a few items. You will find these few items very easy to organize. Problem solved.

Granted, serving prison time as an organizing approach doesn't appeal to everyone. Don't worry. I have equally meritorious ideas.

You might have heard of author Marie Kondo, the organizing guru who decides whether to keep each possession by holding it up and asking, "Does this bring me joy?"

The flaw in that advice: She's asking the wrong question. It's far better to ask, "Does this make me want to scream?"

Based on that criterion alone, I should rid my house of leftover plumbing parts, surplus coffee mugs, books I should have read, gifts I should have regifted, shirts I shouldn't have bought, tools I don't know how to use and the trailer hitch I kept even though I have never had a trailer.

So that will take care of one room.

Still not quite satisfied with my advice? Here's another great organizing idea: move.

Moving forces you to put things in boxes. Send the boxes to a storage facility at least 100 miles away and wait a month. At the end of that period, drive to the storage unit in a small pickup truck with bad suspension and bring back only as much as its aging springs can bear.

Leave the rest of the boxes in storage. Wait for your brain to evolve more. You're welcome.

WE OUGHT TO BEWARE OF AUTO AUTONOMY

Aug. 2, 2016

This self-driving human is not interested in a self-driving car.

Trust an autonomous machine to hurtle me down a freeway at 70 mph? Not happening. I don't even trust the medium-dark setting on the toaster.

Even before Tesla experienced its first self-driving fatality, I was skeptical. Think of all the autonomous programs that already vex us in life:

AutoCorrect, which changes Groveport to Grove Pie and Pickaway County to Pickled Cauliflower. (AutoCorrect is always hungry.)

What if I need to attend a funeral in Tacoma and the self-driving car, in true AutoCorrect fashion, takes me to Taco Bell instead? Grieving relatives will think I forsook their deceased loved one for a 7-Layer Burrito. I can't risk it.

Smartphones, which butt-dial people.

It's always someone you haven't called in years. And, all of a sudden, he's on the line, and what do you say? Do you say, "Sorry, I sat on my phone, felt a pain in my rear and thought of you?" It's awkward.

I don't want a car deciding on its own to drive me to visit an old friend whom I stopped contacting after he shaved his head, joined the Aryan Resistance Front and moved to a concrete bunker in Idaho.

Lawn sprinklers that run in the rain.

I've seen this a million times: Grass being watered automatically—during a thunderstorm.

What that tells me is technology can't even figure out how to come in out of the rain. So I just know that a self-driving convertible would put the top down in a monsoon or run the windshield wipers in a drought.

Aside from these concerns, I think self-driving vehicles will lower self-esteem.

Driving is the one time in life when you feel utterly confident that everyone is an idiot but you. In a challenging world, we need that sense of self-affirmation, not to mention the sweet release of cursing at other drivers.

Where's the fun in cursing at a machine? It's just going to respond with a string of incomprehensible error messages.

Nevertheless, the move toward autonomous cars continues. I'm surprised there's not more of an uproar.

In a car-loving nation awash in conspiracy theories, where's the suspicion of big government taking away our steering wheels? Where's the paranoia about the United Nations plotting to order our cars to transport us to a secret detention camp in the Mojave Desert?

Of course, I fear no such outcome because I know the instant the U.N. enters Mojave Desert into a text window, AutoCorrect will change it to Meringue Dessert.

MEDIA'S TAKE ON SUMMER: HEAT, GERMS AND SHARKS

June 2, 2016

For me, summer officially arrived on Tuesday—when the *Today* show had a story on bacteria in swimming pools.

I know it's summer when the media start warning me about the many ways that the season could kill me.

From now through Labor Day, we can expect an endless string of breathless reports about the dangers of swimming, eating, playing and—in general—living during the summer.

If the heat doesn't desiccate you like a worm on a hot sidewalk, a shark will surely take a bite out of your thigh.

The *Today* report offered a classic of the genre: Correspondent scoops water from various pools and water parks, has it tested and finds germs. How shocking: Who would have ever suspected that, when 500 people are put into a concrete pond, microbes are shed?

Just to make us feel worse, the correspondent pointed out that the one germless pool he found had excessively high levels of chlorine.

So we have a choice between bacterial contamination and chemical poisoning. Isn't summer grand?

Don't get me wrong: I'm not enthusiastic about germy water. You won't see me dipping a baby into a roadside drainage ditch.

As a sun-starved Ohioan, though, I don't want summer's long-awaited delights compromised by overwrought reports about what's breeding in the Jacuzzi.

Let's get some perspective on a few of the other ways that death supposedly awaits us:

Lightning

Yes, I know: A bolt from the heavens could strike me dead. But I'm far more likely to be killed in a traffic crash.

So the golfer pointing a 9-iron at the sky during a thunderstorm might actually be safer than any motorist navigating a stream of texting drivers on a cloudless afternoon.

Shark attacks

Few other things excite cable news as much as a shark attack.

The Florida Museum of Natural History, a keeper of comprehensive statistics on the grave threat, recorded 98 attacks in 2015—in the entire world.

The United States alone averages about 4.5 million dog bites a year.

So, if CNN really wants to scare me, it ought to report breathlessly about every new sighting of a golden retriever.

Heat

I don't dispute that it gets hot in the summer. Nor do I dispute that heat can be dangerous. I merely dispute the notion that being advised to sit in the shade with a glass of ice water counts as groundbreaking information.

Still, as a member of the media, I feel obliged to say: Watch out for poison ivy, use sunscreen, stay hydrated, beware of the Zika virus, avoid riptides, keep away from stinging insects—and have a carefree summer.

HEY, NATURE: WE DESERVE SOME JUSTICE

March 13, 2016

It's time for another edition of Things in Nature That Aren't Fair.

I keep a list in the hope that nature will correct some glaring injustices.

Is it fair that people stranded on a raft in the ocean can't drink the water all around them? Is it fair that female lions do all the work? Is it fair that poison ivy is pretty?

My crusade has made little progress. Nevertheless, here are my latest additions:

An eclipse can blind you.

When the moon moves in front of the sun, an amazing cosmic spectacle is produced. But, if you look at it with an unprotected eye, you damage your vision. That isn't fair.

What's next, nature? An irresistibly fragrant rose that damages your sense of smell? An extremely delicious substance that kills you when you eat it? (Besides doughnuts, I mean.)

Sea turtles lay eggs on land.

The poor things have to swim back to their birthplaces, crawl out of the ocean and laboriously dig holes in the sand with their flippers. And then the hatchlings have to find their way back to the ocean before something eats them.

Why make it so hard? If humans had to crawl to their hometowns to give birth, then leave and hope that the babies find their way to a bus station alone, the species would have been extinct in a couple of generations.

Exercise is the answer to everything.

If I could distill all of the health advice I've ever read into one sentence, it would be this: Keep moving, or you'll die.

Could we get a little balance here? Just once, I'd like to hear a doctor prescribe at least 150 minutes a week of sitting in a recliner.

Sleeping takes work.

First, nature designs us with a sleep requirement. Then it adds all types of complications—nightmares, snoring, 3 a.m. cravings for peanut butter—that make it hard to achieve.

If you demand that we shut down for eight hours a day, nature, at least ensure that the autopilot is reliable.

Sharks keep growing new teeth.

Really, nature? A predator that can rise unseen from the depths and remove my leg in one bite needs an endless tooth supply, too?

Meanwhile, I can lose a molar forever just by chomping on an unpitted olive.

Humans are the weakest primates.

A 120-pound chimpanzee could thrash an NFL linebacker in a bar fight.

Could nature not endow humans with a little more muscle? It might stop us from overcompensating for our frailty by bragging, building McMansions and running for president.

THESE TEAMS IN A LEAGUE OF THEIR OWN

Feb. 7, 2016

After 49 Super Bowls and days of hype about the 50th, I grew bored.

So, rather than join the debates about Peyton Manning's arm strength and Cam Newton's dance moves, I devised some fantasy contests pitting teams outside the world of football. The rules require that the name of each team pair a geographic location with a plural noun.

Here we go:

Bizarre Exercises in Democracy Bowl

Iowa Caucuses vs. New Hampshire Primaries

The first-in-the-nation votes resemble the Super Bowl in that they are scheduled about the same time, attract ridiculous amounts of media coverage and frequently fail to justify their hype.

Non-presidents such as Pat Buchanan, Hillary Clinton, Richard Gephardt, Tom Harkin, Gary Hart and Paul Tsongas are among the victors in past Iowa or New Hampshire voting.

Projected winner: I'm guessing that it won't be the American people.

West Coast Disaster Rumble

San Andreas Faults vs. Santa Ana Winds

An ominous quake-maker goes up against wildfire-fanning winds. If nothing else, the contest proves that California is a really great place to live. Otherwise, why would anyone put up with the constant threat of calamity?

Projected winner: Mother Nature always wins.

World Snack Playoff

Buffalo Wings vs. Philadelphia Cheesesteaks

Inevitably, the game ends in a scoreless tie. Neither side can hold onto the ball because its fingers are too greasy.

Projected winner: cholesterol.

Popular Misconception Duel

Georgia Peaches vs. Wisconsin Dairy Farms

Georgia ranks as only the third-largest producer of peaches, and Wisconsin finishes second to California in dairy production. The Idaho Potatoes were disqualified from the competition because Idaho really does grow the most potatoes.

Projected winner: tourism clichés.

Cheap Beer Championship

Milwaukee's Bests vs. Genesee Cream Ales

The contest can be spun as a higher-education event because it involves two brews that people drink only during college.

Projected winner: No one. The next morning, everyone is a loser.

Mundane Match

Manila Envelopes vs. Portland Cements

Sounds dull, but it would probably outdraw a Blue Jackets game.

Projected winner: the easily entertained.

Hunger Game

Brussels Sprouts vs. Jerusalem Artichokes

If McDonald's sold an Unhappy Meal, these vegetables would probably be added to it.

Projected winner: the Sprouts—because their round shape allows 3-year-olds to throw them farther.

Widely Ignored International Accord Showdown

Geneva Conventions vs. Kyoto Protocols

The game is canceled after it is discovered that the Conventions treat their players inhumanely and the Protocols' private jet burns enormous amounts of fossil fuels.

Projected winner: Armageddon.

IPHONE DOES SO MUCH MORE THAN YOU THOUGHT

Oct. 15, 2015

Every time a new iPhone comes out, so do dozens of articles about all of its hidden functions.

Swipe down from the top to access the hidden "notification drawer," they tell me.

Double-tap a text message and press the hidden "More" tab to forward the message.

Launch the compass (iPhone has a compass?), then swipe right to reveal the bubble level (iPhone has a bubble level?).

And the articles don't even begin to describe all that you can do with the iPhone if you know how to swipe, tap and otherwise manipulate it.

From industry sources who asked to remain fictitious, So To Speak has obtained a list of additional hidden iPhone functions. Here are just a few:

Special delivery

If you dip three fingers in tomato sauce and swipe, the iPhone will have a pizza delivered to your location within 45 minutes.

To add mushrooms, swipe while sitting on a partially decayed log.

Anger management

Want to communicate more assertively? You can instantly convert a diplomatically worded email into a rant in all caps by stabbing at the screen with a middle finger.

To make all your emails look that way, go to "Settings" and activate Donald Trump mode.

Naval maneuvers

It's a little-known fact that taps and swipes on the iPhone correspond to the dots and dashes of Morse code.

The developers of the iPhone didn't realize it themselves until a high-school sophomore, switching rapidly back and forth between apps, inadvertently ordered the U.S. 6th Fleet to blockade the Persian Gulf.

Online shopping

Instead of tediously placing orders on company websites, hidden iPhone functions allow you to make purchases with simple actions:

To order postage stamps, lick the screen.
To buy mosquito repellent, scratch it furiously.
To order Harlem Globetrotters tickets, balance the phone on the tip of an index finger and spin it.

Security safeguard

Using the iPhone in a lead-lined bunker at an undisclosed location while wearing a disguise will automatically send your emails through Hillary Clinton's private server.

Quick getaways

Need to arrange a last-minute flight to, say, Chicago? Simply put the iPhone in airplane mode and fall asleep while sitting upright in a chair with a little bag of peanuts on your lap.

An hour later, you'll wake up with a stiff neck at O'Hare.

NATURE HASN'T BEEN THAT KIND

May 19, 2015

Welcome to another edition of Things in Nature That Aren't Fair.

It marks my recurring attempt to point out injustices in the natural order—Exhibit A being that carbon monoxide is colorless and odorless.

A poisonous gas you can't see or smell? That isn't fair.

I also think nature dealt salmon a raw deal when it designed them to swim upstream for hundreds of miles so they can have sex just once and then die.

Here are the latest additions to my list:

Termites eat wood.

Of all the things that a termite could eat in a house, why does it have to be wood? A termite that ate aluminum siding or '90s wallpaper would actually beautify the nation while leaving houses structurally sound.

And who hasn't longed for some type of insect to develop a taste for political yard signs or Lands' End catalogs?

Poison ivy looks harmless.

A plant that turns people into walking pustules should be required to provide a signal of its menace. But poison ivy has innocuous-looking foliage, attractive berries and ravishing fall color. Worse, it grows everywhere.

Clearly, nature has given poison ivy an outrageous advantage—for which our only defenses are long pants and Roundup.

Nothing cures a hangover.

College sophomores will tell you they have the ultimate hangover remedy—which is proof enough that no remedy exists. Nor am I asking for one.

I'm merely asking that such a painful condition at least have the decency to know when to quit.

I'm not arguing for painless drinking, because, if it were, the entire nation would be sloshed most of the time. I'm saying that after a decent interval of suffering—perhaps an hour on a weekday and two on a weekend—the point has been made, and it's time for nature to let up.

Salamanders grow new legs.

They don't drive motorcycles or use chain saws, so I'm not sure how often salamanders even lose a leg.

But, when they do, it's no problem: They just grow another one.

In a fairer world, humans would have that ability. We're the ones with wood chippers and augers and other things that threaten to remove body parts. What was nature thinking?

Dolphins practice half-brain sleep.

OK, nature, I can see why allowing a marine mammal to put half its brain to sleep at a time was a good idea. Otherwise, the poor thing would drown.

Would it have been too much to extend the ability to humans? Just about every office worker in America is running at half-brain capacity after lunch, anyway.

If nature can recognize the hazards of sleeping underwater, it should understand the challenge of staying awake during a 3 p.m. PowerPoint presentation.

BRAWNY DINO IN A CLASS BY ITSELF

April 12, 2015

Biggest comeback of the year so far?

No, it isn't Alex Rodriguez taking the field again for the New York Yankees.

Nor is it Carly Rae Jepsen releasing a new song.

It's the pending return of the brontosaurus, the dinosaur with the coolest name among animals, extinct or otherwise.

What kid growing up in the '50s and '60s could possibly resist a mountainous beast whose name evokes the idea of brawn and is translated as "thunder lizard"?

By then, scientists had been saying for decades that the brontosaurus had been misidentified as a separate species and was really a type of apatosaurus. But the brontosaurus name hung on through my childhood for several reasons:

- The Flintstones ate brontosaurus burgers, and Sinclair Oil used the creature as a symbol for its gas stations.
- *The Giant Golden Book of Dinosaurs and Other Prehistoric Reptiles,* a sumptuously illustrated 1960 work, fascinated a lot of kids.
- The book had a bloody rendering of an allosaurus digging its claws into the flanks of a brontosaurus. No 6-year-old boy could resist it.
- Most dinosaur names are wretched. For every velociraptor (cool name), there are 10 therizinosauruses (name that sounds like a prehistoric prescription drug).

And scientists were telling me to give up brontosaurus for the colorless apatosaurus? Outrageous.

Well, brontosaurus might be back.

The media (ruled by former Flintstones watchers of my age) went wild last week over word that a new study of dinosaur skeletons has concluded that the thunder lizard really was a species distinct from the apatosaurus.

The name brontosaurus was coined in the 1870s to describe a long-necked, plant-eating behemoth whose bones had been dug up in Wyoming.

A brontosaurus skeleton that went on display in 1905 at the American Museum of Natural History in New York electrified the public.

By then, some scientists were already saying the name was wrong, but not until the 1970s and '80s did apatosaurus really begin to supplant it.

The first-grader in me has always rebelled at that development.

I was so enraptured by dinosaurs at age 6 that people thought I was going to be a paleontologist. But I had no scientific inclinations. What I loved were the names. I'd walk around spelling tyrannosaurus, diplodocus and triceratops for anyone within earshot.

I'd find it highly satisfying to have the thunder lizard's name back in the official lineup. But I never felt I needed science's guidance on what to call a 30-ton animal with bridge-abutment legs.

It has always been brontosaurus to me.

ITALIAN APP LEADS TO STRANGE STATEMENTS

Feb. 24, 2015

I intend to visit Italy one of these days, so I'm trying to expand my Italian vocabulary.

Owing to my ancestry, I know many Italian curse words. If I hit my thumb with a hammer in Florence, I should be able to communicate with the native population. Beyond that, I am limited to gesturing and adding extraneous vowels to English words.

But I'm working on it—I think.

I've discovered the smartphone app Duolingo, which purports to make one fluent in Italian—if fluent means being able to say things such as "The penguin eats fruit."

I love the way it sounds ("Il pinguino mangia frutta"), but I'm not sure how useful the sentence would be when asking for directions in Rome. (Nor am I sure where Duolingo got its information on penguin nutrition.)

I can also say "My shoes are blue" and "The woman buys a red sweater" in Italian. I was pretty impressed with myself until I looked at the sentences objectively and realized they sound like code phrases between spies in a World War II movie.

To be sure, I've also practiced more useful sentences such as "Where is the bathroom?" and "How much do I owe?" But they don't stick in my head as readily as animals and colors.

So let's say I need a doctor in Naples. Under pressure, I fear I'll just grasp at the first Duolingo words that come to mind and say, "I gave my pants to the yellow duck."

Also, I'm addicted to the app—which makes me think it might just be a video game. It certainly has gamelike qualities, such as challenges I have to conquer to accumulate points and enter higher levels.

I should probably stop judging people who spend hours trying to get Tiffi through the licorice swirls in Candy Crush Saga. They could fire right back with "Oh, yeah, and you spend hours learning to say 'They are not my cows' in Italian."

I'm a little suspicious of the whole self-improvement-by-smartphone movement because it isn't painful enough. Learning Italian should involve struggling with long lists of Italian verbs, not using my thumbs to choose the correct translation of "I have blue pockets."

Even exercise, which is supposed to hurt, is easier as presented by a phone app.

Which explains my other app addiction: 7 Minute Workout.

That's right: seven minutes.

Supposedly there is scientific research behind it, but, if I wanted to make an exercise app popular, I'd certainly lean toward less pain. If you want a guaranteed loser, try titling one "The 2-Hour Fitness Ordeal."

Despite my skepticism, I use 7 Minute Workout when I'm in a hurry.

Afterward, I congratulate myself with a stirring Italian phrase such as "La cipolla e una verdura" ("The onion is a vegetable").

ALTERNATIVES TO ROSES A BIT THORNY

Feb. 12, 2015

Red roses say love.

Otherwise, sources differ on what various types and colors of flowers symbolize.

Just in time for Valentine's Day, I am stepping in to confuse matters further.

I'll let other experts deal with orchids, carnations and other predictable buds. I'm interested in more unconventional choices.

So here is Joe's Guide to Flowers for Less-Committed Relationships (as always, proceed with caution):

Dandelion

Description: a hardy broadleaf weed whose yellow flowers pockmark even the most carefully tended lawns in the spring.

Message: Thank you for being the bright little blossom that adds a colorful note of spontaneity to my carefully planned life. No matter how often you disrupt my tightly organized schedule, I will try to resist the urge to spray you with Roundup.

Apt recipient: an urban forager who, even if less than thrilled by the bouquet, might think, "Well, at least I can throw it in a salad."

Poinsettia

Description: a plant whose red and green foliage makes it a popular choice at Christmastime but one that usually looks bad by Valentine's Day.

Message: In the first flush of our relationship, I was attracted to your beauty. Even though you have since turned pale and sickly, I will not abandon you. Instead, I will stick you in a closet because I think I remember my aunt doing that.

Apt recipient: someone who isn't claustrophobic.

Venus' flytrap

Description: a carnivorous plant with leaves that snap shut, trapping insects that are then digested for nourishment.

Message: You have lured me with your charms, and I am as hopelessly entangled in your affections as a beetle trapped by the hair-like protrusions of a plant native to the subtropical wetlands of the Carolinas.

Apt recipients: botanists or fans of horror stories, as long as you check to ensure they aren't vegetarians.

Eastern skunk cabbage

Description: a native wildflower that blooms in February and attracts insects with its odor.

Message: Your love motivated me to go to a state nature preserve and dig up some weeds that smell bad. Don't read too much into it.

Apt recipient: someone who won't report you to the Ohio Department of Natural Resources and isn't armed.

Money plant

Description: a biennial that produces round, silvery seedpods that resemble coins.

Message: Let this plant symbolize my eagerness to spend any amount of money for the right to whisper in your ear, flatter you with praise and beg for your favors.

Apt recipients: members of Congress.

WITHOUT NICKNAMES, WEATHER JUST GRAY

Nov. 11, 2014

It's only mid-November, and winter-weather hype has already reached ridiculous proportions.

The cold spell we're supposed to have this week used to be called just that: a cold spell.

Now, it's a polar vortex. Why? The media love to hype weather by creating nicknames that suggest something ominous. Even in central Ohio, where "partly cloudy" describes the weather most of the year, we are constantly assaulted by Alberta Clippers and Siberian Expresses.

I predict that more of the unremarkable conditions will get new nicknames, too.

To get in on the fun, I've prepared a glossary:

Old name: scattered frost

New name: Arctic killer glaze

Lethal to tender plants, it also destroys careers by making people late for work because they didn't anticipate having to scrape the windshield.

NFL cheerleaders have to jiggle with extra urgency to avoid hypothermia.

Old name: gusty winds

New name: Siberian howler

It descends from the tundra at speeds of 20 to 30 mph, obliterating carefully raked piles of leaves and plastering fast-food wrappers against fences in a fearsome display of might.

In the face of such fury, mothers race to put sweaters on children, and smokers struggle desperately with lighters.

Old name: snow flurries

New name: concentrated flake outburst

Known by weather experts as a CFO, the phenomenon quickly turns a gray subfreezing day into a gray subfreezing day with light snow.

A particularly intense CFO has been known to whiten lawns, moisten sidewalks and inspire youngsters to scrape snow from every nearby surface in a futile effort to gather enough to build a fort.

Old name: patchy fog

New name: shroud of doom

When the dreaded haze descends over a low-lying area, motorists flip on their headlights and slow down to 75 mph.

Commuters miss their breakfast burritos because the Taco Bell freeway sign was too obscured by mist. Tormented by hunger, they resort to vending-machine doughnuts. The resulting blood-sugar spike and crash leave them sluggish and unmotivated. So they spend the day watching Internet cat videos, costing the economy millions of dollars in lost productivity.

Old name: overcast skies

New name: winter murk storm

Leaden skies smother central Ohio in gray, causing residents to question the very existence of the sun. To pass the time, they dream of summer heat waves—which will henceforth be called "equatorial temperature invasions."

WHEN POT IS LEGAL HERE, IT WILL NEED COOL NAMES

July 8, 2014

Washington joins Colorado today as a state where recreational marijuana is sold legally.

It might be a long time before Ohio does likewise, but that just gives us more time to develop the all-important branding strategy.

I've been researching the matter because we'll need names for the different strains of Ohio pot. The words black, green, thunder, haze and cannabis are among those that recur frequently in pot names in Colorado, but I think we have room to expand that vocabulary and give it an Ohio spin.

Here are some Ohio pot strains I envision:

Green Ribbon

A favorite in agricultural circles, Green Ribbon is usually deep-fried and consumed on a stick. It smells like a corn dog with hints of barnyard animal and cotton candy.

Users say it makes them feel as if they're on the Tilt-A-Whirl even when they aren't.

Bigfoot

Only a few people claim to have ever seen the foul-smelling but immensely powerful strain—and they were hallucinating.

Nevertheless, those who believe that it exists have regular gatherings where they pore over grainy photos that could be the elusive plant—or could be an office palm dragged into a clearing in woods near Akron.

Potluck

It smells like green-bean casserole and makes people ravenously hungry for seven-layer salad and coleslaw.

Users sometimes get so high that they go home without their Tupperware containers.

Utica Thunderfrack

It smells like money.

Some people say it makes the earth move beneath their feet.

State legislators are so stoned on it that they can't protect the public interest. In fact, they can't even remember where they put it.

Amish Black

This strain has a profoundly mellowing effect. Tourists who smoke it think they're experiencing a quaint 19th-century lifestyle while navigating the heavy traffic, crowded flea markets and side-by-side gift shops of Holmes County.

Gahannabis

A mood elevator, it causes people who live in Gahanna to feel like they live in New Albany.

Scarlet Haze

Consumed year-round in central Ohio, it ignites intense feelings of religious devotion and an obsessive interest in the 40-yard-dash times of teenagers.

Users often experience alternating episodes of euphoria and anxiety, particularly on autumn Saturdays.

When mixed with alcohol, it can cause obnoxiousness to rise to toxic levels.

South Grass Island

When smoked on Memorial Day, this potent blend causes a high lasting all summer.

BOOMERS HOLD TIGHT TO LABELS OF YOUTH

February 27, 2014

I detect heavy baby-boomer influence in a new survey of what Americans think about aging.

People in their 50s said a person isn't old until 68. People in their 60s said 73. That's classic baby-boomer denial.

People in their 70s, who aren't boomers, were willing to concede that 75 is old. The average life expectancy is 78, so they narrowly avoided the embarrassment of declaring only the dead to be old. The boomers won't be as astute.

The survey was done for the magazine published by the AARP, which used to stand for the American Association of Retired Persons until that started sounding too old. The organization really should know better than to expect truthful baby-boomer answers to questions such as "How would others describe you based on your age?"

The most popular response was "younger," followed by "active and healthy" and "in the prime of life." If "fresh-faced icon of strength, intelligence and sexual energy" had been an option, I'm sure that it would have finished right up there.

My fellow baby boomers are never going to admit they're old. They might agree to "mature" on a day when their knees are acting up, but that's as far as they'll go. They'll just keep moving the goal posts on "elderly" until 105-year-old boomers are claiming they don't expect to enter that category until 107.

But here's the thing, boomers: The age category that America worships is called "young," not "surprisingly well-preserved." And we aren't passing for young.

The young have distinct characteristics that can't be faked. As I've noted before, one of the most important is this: The young actually have to be in motion to get hurt. If you can injure yourself sitting awkwardly in a chair, you aren't young.

Also, any boomer with children should know that the young aren't fooled by our strenuous efforts to deny aging. Being young, they have great eyesight, for one thing. For another, they're smart enough to realize that their boomer parents come up short on key markers of youth: musical preferences, body-mass index, texting speed, ability to stay up until 3 a.m.

So, if the young aren't buying it, who is left for us to try to fool? Two groups:

- People 70 and older—but that's a wasted effort because we've seemed young to them since we were born.
- Ourselves.

Ah, we've arrived at the true target of the effort. It turns out that all the face-lifts, hair dyes, erectile-dysfunction drugs and sports cars are really aimed at convincing one another that we maintain the bloom of youth.

And surveys show that it's working.

L.A.: THE CITY INTO WHICH WE ALL FIT

Nov. 3, 2011

The 7 billionth human was born on Monday, we're told.

It's an astounding number, but here's an equally astounding fact: All 7 billion of us, standing shoulder to shoulder, would fit within the city of Los Angeles, according to *National Geographic.*

From that, I can draw only one conclusion: We should have a convention—all 7 billion of us—in L.A. before numbers make it unwieldy. (The 8 billionth human is a mere 14 years away. Imagine what that would do to L.A. traffic.)

I've written the opening address already:

"Welcome, people of Earth, to the first Global Convention. With the entire population of the world gathered here, I think I can safely say that never in the history of humanity has there been a better networking opportunity.

"Sorry we're running a little late, but it takes a while to get 7 billion people through security. Anyone who had weapons confiscated at the gate can pick them up at the end of the day. They are in bins, organized by category: rocks, knives, blowguns, small arms, automatic weapons, explosives, helicopter gunships, aircraft carriers, etc. Thank you for your cooperation.

"Before we get started, I have a few housekeeping announcements.

"We'd like to encourage mingling during the noon break, so, after picking up your box lunches, please sit in this order:

"People prone to complain that the turkey sandwich doesn't have meat from free-range birds will sit with people who plan to save the sandwich wrappings to plug holes in the cardboard hovels where they live with 19 family members.

"Vegans will sit with people who survive on grubs and beetles.

"Rugged individualists who never got a handout in their lives and are sick and tired of people thinking society owes them a living will sit with orphans who live on garbage piles in Third World countries.

"You all should have a packet listing the various programs and classes we have planned for the day. I need to make note of a couple of changes. I'm sorry to announce that the following sessions are full: 'Erotic Art From Around the World,' 'How To Get Rich Without Leaving Your House' and 'Chocolate for All Latitudes.'

"We have plenty of room in these sessions: 'Our Vanishing Ecosystems,' 'Medicines That Could Save Millions Right Now' and 'Water: The Global Crisis That Can't Wait.'

"OK, I think a nice way to begin this historic gathering would be to shake hands with the person next to you. If you can't shake hands with the person next to you because of religious or cultural prohibitions, then just smile. If you can't smile because of historical enmity between your ancestors, then just refrain from killing each other.

"Remember, our goal for the day is to begin to think of each other not as faceless rivals or anonymous enemies but as unique individuals who all belong to one big family.

"Please help us with this task by wearing your name tag at all times."

HE CAN'T STASH OR TRASH HIS CLUTTER

Jan. 24, 2010

The month is almost half gone, and I have yet to unclutter.

Everyone vows to unclutter when a new year begins. I didn't make a formal vow this year, but I held uncluttering in my mind as an ideal to be pursued, like world peace.

What keeps me from achieving the dream? I think it's the counterintuitive nature of the struggle against clutter. It's a little bit like fighting an insurgency: Sometimes bringing all your power to bear simply makes the situation worse.

I used to think that no clutter could withstand the heavy weaponry of storage space. But I have come to realize that clutter loves storage space because it hints at weakness on the part of the enemy.

A man who converts the space over his garage into an attic is not signaling his resolve to eradicate clutter. He is signaling that he lacks the will to rid himself of the bunk beds his kids haven't used since the Clinton administration. He will, instead, store the beds, disassembled, because you never know—the day could come when he wants to open a summer camp.

To store clutter is to be defeated by clutter. You haven't gotten rid of it; you've just moved it, leaving behind a vacuum that will be filled by—guess what?—more clutter.

Knowing this, why don't I just get rid of it?

No. 1, I'm married. One of the rules of marriage is that it's always the other person's stuff that's clutter. Your stuff consists of priceless artifacts, sentimental objects, useful material and uncategorized stuff whose true value will become apparent only in an emergency.

If the Chinese ever invade, the rest of you might surrender, but I'll fight them off with my stock of old curtain rods, outdated electronic devices and half-full cans of paint. Mark my words.

Multiply this attitude by two for a couple, and you can see why things pile up.

The second reason I can't get rid of stuff: guilt.

I can't throw away anything with a clear conscience these days. TVs? They're full of hazardous materials. Ugly plastic flowerpots? They'll lie in the landfill for 6 billion years. A bicycle no one rides? Some kid should have it.

The impulse to donate, recycle or reuse is a noble one, but it stands in the way of uncluttering. Instead of throwing away clutter, I gather it up and move it to the garage, where it remains while I search for a charitable organization in desperate need of a small appliance that doesn't work.

The third obstacle to getting rid of clutter is that some clutter actually serves a purpose. Books that were last read two decades ago still pull duty as decorative objects.

Furthermore, I'm always afraid that if I get rid of a book, I'll forget that I consumed its knowledge. I like passing by a shelf, catching a glimpse of *Art of the Western World* or *The Reader's Digest Fix-It-Yourself Manual* and being reminded that I know something about Renaissance painting and toilet flush mechanisms, although I can't quite remember what.

So it's an endless battle. But give up? Never. I'll fight clutter to my dying day. And then? My heirs will have a big garage sale.

EVOLUTION WARNS US: RUN FOR YOUR LIFE

Sept. 4, 2008

Until further notice, running is the best exercise.

If you hate to run, don't fret. A study will soon come out to contradict the study that touted running. Conflicting exercise advice is a staple of American culture.

The study on running, by Stanford University researchers, has enjoyed wide circulation in the media. "Running is the fountain of youth," the headlines inevitably said.

The study said nothing of the sort. It said that ancient runners have fewer health problems than ancient nonrunners. They get less heart disease and cancer. They age slower. Their joints work better despite the pounding. But they're still ancient.

The fixation on youth was no doubt supplied by the baby boomers who manage the media. They can't let go of the notion that someday, somehow, someone is going to find a way to make it 1968 again.

I've pretty much given up on that idea. I look at exercise as a holding action. The clock is always going to tick, but if a few push-ups and some gallops around the neighborhood make it tick slower, I'm all for it.

Still, a little agreement on what works would be nice.

Exercise advice seems to swing between two poles: At one extreme, they tell you that you need four hours of mountain-climbing, marathon-running and swimming in an icy river to stay healthy. At the other, they tell you that moderate activity—say 15 minutes of foot-jiggling in front of the television twice a week—can be surprisingly beneficial.

Both things can't be true. Come on people, focus: What's going to keep me prancing around the nursing home at 85?

With no definitive answer to that question, I try to resolve the disparities in exercise advice by taking evolution into account.

Do I figure that my ancestors survived on Earth by running or by taking leisurely strolls in the woods while saber-toothed tigers and warlike tribes of cannibals roamed around looking for people to eat?

I'm going with running. My guess is that our bodies evolved to run for survival and, therefore, it makes sense that it would remain therapeutic today. We were built to do it.

I wish this weren't true, because running for exercise is a miserable activity. I know people talk about the "runner's high" and all that, but the only high I get out of it comes from stopping. Too bad our ancestors didn't learn to survive by playing croquet.

On the other hand, I like the simplicity of running. Just go outside and move your legs fast. If the point is to efficiently work yourself into a state of exhaustion, running accomplishes that in minutes, with no annual fees.

It also has a primitive cachet. It's the exercise equivalent of the stone-age diet of whole grains, nuts and seeds. I can imagine myself on the savanna, running from beasts, grubbing for nutrients and wishing for all the world that someone would hurry up and invent tranquilizer darts and pizza.

Apart from all that, I have to consider this: At my age (54), if I stop running, I might seize up and be unable to start again.

OHIO CRITTERS BOAST TALENTS WORTHY OF TV

March 25, 2007

Animals in Ohio deserve way more media exposure than they get.

I'm reminded of this each spring, when rabbits defy dogs and fences to nibble gardens to death.

Elsewhere, squirrels are breaking into attics, raccoons are opening unopenable trash cans and deer are crossing I-270 to get to the best shrubs.

And how about Canada geese? They actually seize suburban property without due process. Not even county commissioners can do that.

In short, Ohio animals are courageous, resourceful and stealthy.

Yet they get no love from *Nature* or Animal Planet, or any of the other fang-and-fin shows and networks that fixate on the same overrated creatures episode after episode.

I like crocodiles as much as the next guy, but come on: What kind of a self-respecting predator has jaws that can be held shut by duct tape?

Try that with an Ohio raccoon. It will remove the tape, wrap it back onto the roll and return it to the Home Depot for a refund. Raccoons are far more clever than crocodiles.

These creatures also make my list of animals that get too much publicity:

Cheetahs. Yes, I know: They're pretty, and they can run 70 mph. But they get tired so quickly that their prey often gets away.

This frustrates me. When is it going to occur to them to slow down to 55 mph, wait for the gazelle to exhaust itself, then sit down to lunch?

If Ohio groundhogs wasted energy the way cheetahs do, they'd have coal mines for burrows.

Sharks. Imagine an Ohio squirrel happening on a few hundred delicious crocus bulbs. Does he bite one and run away? No. He takes the whole collection.

Sharks? Not that smart. Consider: Beachgoers are the crocus bulbs of the shark world. Yet, year after year, we hear about a shark that takes a bite out of a swimmer or two and abruptly leaves.

Wouldn't you think this overpublicized "eating machine" would figure out that tourists, especially the high-fat American kind, offer the same caloric content as elephant seals at a fraction of the risk?

Ostriches. Wow, did they mess up.

They surrendered the power of flight so they could grow to 250 pounds and strut imperiously—as if Superman decided he'd rather be Dr. Phil.

And then what happened? They became ranch animals. You'd never catch an Ohio cardinal taking that deal.

Salmon. This business of swimming upstream to reproduce—isn't it just a bit much?

We all want to honor our heritage, but at some point you have to ask yourself what's worse: laying eggs in a strange neighborhood or swimming into the gaping maw of a grizzly bear?

Our geese are far more practical than salmon. You don't see them flying all the way to Canada anymore, because they know they can build a nest around any retention pond in Westerville.

Pandas. A telegenic animal that wears fur and eats nothing but bamboo shoots? Please. It sounds like a four-legged version of Nicole Richie.

Ohio deer are cute, too, but you won't catch them turning up their pretty noses at other forms of vegetation.

I wish the media would do more to glamorize our deer. For one thing, it might distract them from eating my backyard.

WHAT GOES AROUND (SNIFF), COMES AROUND

Jan. 8. 2006

"There's something going around." During an Ohio winter, this statement is always true. Half the population is coughing, sneezing and hacking its way through January.

We leave little trails of mucus, like slugs with earmuffs.

But "There's something going around" is more than just an obvious statement. It's a vital phrase in the etiquette of minor illness, a code of behavior in which Ohioans are well-versed.

What about those who are newly arrived from California or Hawaii, or someplace else where people don't spend the period from Thanksgiving to Easter cooped up in a germ-laden shelter? For them, I've prepared this guide to contagious courtesy:

- When someone complains of illness, you must respond with the right mixture of concern and hope. Hence, "There's something going around" acknowledges the illness yet reassures the sufferer that it's a common malady unlikely to lead to uncontrollable bleeding, paralysis and death.

  Plus, it's short. You don't want to spend too much time talking to a disease vector.

- People around here often say "I have a virus" but never "I have bacteria." It's just not done, I suspect because bacteria sounds germier and less hygienic. Listeners might think you need a bath.

- You can't go wrong blaming the weather. Even though science proved several centuries ago that microbes make us sick, the weather here is so vexing that people refuse to absolve it of responsibility.

Ohioans are especially suspicious of temperature fluctuations. You might think a 50-degree reading in January would cause widespread rejoicing.

Instead, the temperature prompts dark warnings about "flu weather." This is the meteorological equivalent of being afraid to get too happy during Ohio State football season because a heartbreaking loss might lie just ahead.

- It's always polite to recommend a folk remedy for colds. Zinc tablets, vitamin C, herbs, the latest over-the-counter miracle spray—any of these can be offered. One need only listen for sounds of communal wheezing to know that such remedies don't work. But think of them as pharmaceutical flowers offered to lift spirits, if not white blood cell counts.

  Try to restrict your recommendations to substances that sound like medicine. People who are sick will become suspicious if you claim you ward off colds by drinking three margaritas a day before dinner.

- Calling in sick with a cold demands delicate timing. You're more contagious early but display more obvious symptoms later. So it's a matter of choosing between high contagion and high drama.

  Most people seem to go for the drama, which is why some offices have been passing around the same cold since 1965.

- "Stomach flu" technically does not exist, but don't count on that to stop you from getting it. It's a malady that carries with it an ironclad right to privacy. Once you say you have it, no one will pry for details.

- Given that hands are the leading transmitters of cold germs, it would actually be more polite to decline a handshake rather than accept it.

  But Ohioans are too courteous to practice that kind of politeness. Hence, "there is always something going around."

STEREOTYPES EXPLAIN LITTLE ABOUT PEOPLE IN THE WORKPLACE

Oct. 16, 2016

I'm a baby boomer, which—if you believe media stereotypes—makes me a different species from members of the millennial generation.

Recently, I've noticed that, after years of churning out stories about baby boomers struggling to manage millennials in the workplace, the media have turned the tables: Millennials are now being advised on how to manage baby boomers. (Generation X figures in there, too, but let's not complicate matters.)

In both cases, the generations are presumed to fit into neat categories. The meeting of the two is then presented as akin to an encounter between modern city dwellers and a primitive Amazon tribe, with workplace consultants brought in for advice on how to bridge the cultural divide.

Here's an excerpt from a *Los Angeles Times* article on how millennials must beware of insulting boomers:

> "Older colleagues may drop comments such as, 'I have children your age!' Under no circumstance should you point out that you have parents their age. Just smile and don't stop smiling for the duration of your employment."

Otherwise, they might attack you with their crudely fashioned war clubs.

In 2003, the *St. Petersburg Times* published an article telling boomer bosses how to appease those exotic millennials:

> "Turn-offs are nasty bosses, inflexible hours and a work atmosphere that is not fun. Turn-ons include friendly co-workers,

understanding bosses, personal recognition, benefits and tuition reimbursement."

Millennials like pleasant work environments? Will we ever understand these mysterious savages?

Inevitably, the articles arrive at the big reveal, where a consultant sagely passes on what should be obvious to any sentient being: In workplaces, people have to communicate.

If boomers, speaking their throwback hippie slang, and millennials, chattering in Brooklyn hipster, can just find a way to communicate—perhaps by hand gesture?—all will be well.

Who would have thought?

As for the future, well, keep in mind that generational stereotypes are fluid.

In workplace articles, boomers—who were all presumed to be anti-authoritarian partyers when young—now are assigned the role of aging, career-obsessed toilers. The millennials are the ones portrayed as the live-for-today types hopping from job to job.

Do you suppose that could have anything to do with life stage? There's a reason we call marriage, kids and mortgages "settling down."

So, here's an easy prediction: A decade or so from now, consultants will be making money by advising aging millennial executives on how to accommodate the alien ways of a new generation.

And the answer won't be any different.

THE BAD ROMANTIC ADVICE IN CHRISTMAS CAROLS

Dec. 24, 2015

Today's topic: why you shouldn't take your dating advice from Christmas songs.

That is, besides "Baby, It's Cold Outside"—the poster song for unacceptable behavior, with its suggestion of drink doctoring.

I mean holiday tunes whose lyrics wouldn't land you in court but could mean a lot of lonely nights if you took them too literally.

Let's begin with "Winter Wonderland." ("Sleigh bells ring; are you listenin'?")

I get the general premise: leisurely walk, ringing sleigh bells, glistening snow. It sounds romantic, if a little cold.

Even the part about building a snowman in a meadow doesn't seem too bad.

But pretending that he is Parson Brown? Let's take a step back.

You've already dragged your special someone into a field on a cold night. And now, impulsively, you want to propose marriage officiated by an imaginary figure? Will the best man be a scarecrow, just to complete the theme?

Let's move on to "Let It Snow! Let It Snow! Let It Snow!" ("Oh, the weather outside is frightful, but the fire is so delightful.")

Again, it starts well: snowy night, flickering flames, just the two of you. It sounds cozy.

And I find it commendable that you planned ahead and brought a sensual delight for your love interest—nice touch.

So what is it? Well, according to the song, it's popcorn—seriously.

So let's review: You decided that the best way to impress a date was not with a bottle of wine or some strawberries dipped in chocolate. You passed by those reliable symbols of affection and went straight for a bag of Orville Redenbacher's?

Gee, how will you top that on the second date? Chex Mix?

Even holiday favorites that don't present overtly romantic scenarios carry risks.

Let's say you wanted to mimic the quietly festive mood of "The Christmas Song." Good idea? I'm not so sure.

Let's take it line by line:

Chestnuts roasting on an open fire: The fire is good. The chestnuts are a little 19th-century, but no harm done.

Jack Frost nipping at your nose: Really? You turned the thermostat down to the point that frostbite is possible?

Yuletide carols being sung by a choir: Wait, what? Into this romantic setting, you invited a 56-voice ensemble to belt out "Deck the Halls"?

And folks dressed up like Eskimos: That's it—the mood of intimacy is dead, even if they leave their sled dogs outside.

Could you redeem yourself with the turkey and mistletoe in the next verse? Doubtful.

By then, I suspect, your date will have long since said, "Have yourself a merry little Christmas" and gone home.

SMART TOILET SOUNDS LIKE A DUMB IDEA

Dec. 20, 2016

Here's an idea whose time will never come, at least for me: the smart toilet.

A BBC story I read recently said that a Japanese company has a $12,000 model with, among other features, a remote control that sends a robot arm sliding beneath the user with adjustable water jets.

No, thank you. Robot arms are just not welcome in certain areas. I've learned from bitter experience not to place too much trust in automatic processes.

I have a car heater that decides on its own when I'm too warm and a garage door opener that calls in sick when the temperature drops below 20 degrees. While annoying, they do not carry the tragic potential of a robot toilet gone rogue.

Even if the injury weren't fatal, you'd die of embarrassment in the emergency room.

Besides, having been through any number of routine technology failures, I never, ever, want to hear this sentence, "The toilet won't start."

The BBC reports that another Japanese company (the Japanese are on the cutting edge of bathroom tech) has a toilet with a Bluetooth connection so that you can direct its various functions via smartphone.

If you thought hackers meddling in our presidential election was worrisome, just imagine them gaining control of our toilets. It would give new meaning to the term Wikileaks.

The smart toilet is part of that "Internet of Things" thing, in which everyday objects get sensors, regardless of whether they need them. Trash cans, diapers, clothespins, forks, bras and chopsticks—there's a long list of everyday objects that are now thinking for themselves.

The website www.weputachipinit.tumblr.com keeps a running list of some of the more ridiculous examples.

Don't get me wrong: I don't oppose progress. But the people behind the new wonder toilets are putting the focus in the wrong place, if you ask me.

What's been one of the most disruptive uses of technology in recent years? Uber. A phone app took something that hadn't changed in decades—the cab ride—and revolutionized it.

And what's the one thing that when you need it, you really, really need it? A toilet.

So, obviously, what the world—or at least the beer-drinking regions—needs is an Uber toilet. Simply tap an app on your smartphone and within minutes, a portable potty appears. (It might be a self-propelled, driverless potty; I haven't worked out the details yet.)

Forget selling $12,000 smart toilets. When the situation is urgent enough, there are people who would pay good money just to use a dumb one.

HAD TO SAY IT

LAUREATES NEED SONGS POWERED BY DYLAN

Oct. 20, 2016

I'm OK with Bob Dylan winning the Nobel Prize for Literature, but I think the Nobel committee missed an opportunity.

It should have had Dylan write songs for the other Nobel winners.

Having the Nobel medal hanging from your neck is quite an honor, but how often does a physicist or chemist get the opportunity to be the subject of a Dylan song?

Although I can't know for sure, I think Dylan would have written something like this:

"Mr. Tiny Machine Man"
(*To the tune of "Mr. Tambourine Man"*)

Written for: Jean-Pierre Sauvage, J. Fraser Stoddart and Bernard L. Feringa, who won the Nobel Prize in chemistry for figuring out how to control the movements of molecules so they can make microscopic machines.

Hey, Mr. Tiny Machine Man
Make a tool for me,
A micro-vac to suction out my sinuses
Hey Mr. Tiny Machine Man
Clear my allergy,
And in the jingle-jangle morning I won't sneeze upon you

"Glowin' on Your Chest"
(*To the tune of "Blowin' in the Wind"*)

Written for: David J. Thouless, F. Duncan M. Haldane and J. Michael Kosterlitz, who won the physics prize for using advanced mathematical methods to study unusual phases of matter.

How many slackers once called you a nerd
When with calculus textbooks you sat?
Yes, and how many times have you smirked at them since
When they ask if you want fries with that?
Yes, and how many A-lists have added your name?
Why does Colbert say stop by and chat?
The reason, my friend, is glowin' on your chest
The reason is glowin' on your chest.

"Like a Lysosome"

(To the tune of "Like a Rolling Stone")

Written for: Yoshinori Ohsumi, the scientist who won the Nobel in medicine for important discoveries about "autophagy," a process by which a cell "eats itself," destroying its components and sending them to a recycling compartment called a lysosome. It's believed to play an essential role in bodily processes.

Once upon a time you were less than fine,
So by design on yourself you dined, didn't you?
You said, "Gotta beautify, tell my cells bye-bye, get a new supply,
I'm not kiddin' you."
You finally figured out
How to make a turnabout
All the nasty to knock out
Free of dandruff, now, no doubt
But what an ordeal.
Tell me how does it feel?
How does it feel?
To recycle skin and bone?
Nose hair and kidney stone?
Like a lysosome
Like a lysosome.

KIDS' TALES REIMAGINED FOR THE WORLD WE KNOW NOW

Feb. 2, 2017

I think we need to rewrite some classic children's book now that we live in the Age of Trump.

Here are a few proposals:

Wizard of Ostracism

For the second time, a tornado blows Dorothy to the Land of Oz, where she learns that the Munchkins have imposed a temporary travel ban on immigrants and refugees.

"Your gingham dress and pigtails frighten us," the Munchkin mayor explains. "You'll have to catch the next tornado home."

"But you were such a welcoming people last time," Dorothy replies. "All that singing and dancing. What happened?"

"It's a dangerous world out there," the mayor says. "We have to protect our magical land."

"I think the magic's gone, dude," Dorothy replies.

Where the Constitution Ends

(A rewrite of Shel Silverstein's poem "Where the Sidewalk Ends")

There is a place where the Constitution ends, and it's where fear begins,
And there the threats get overinflated, and there the truth gets stretched and shaded,
And the Bill of Rights gets desiccated and drifts away in the wind.

Where the Wild Things Aren't

A young boy sets off on an imaginary journey by boat to the land of the wild things.

When he gets there, he finds that rising seas levels have prompted all the wild things to leave.

Max roars his terrible roars and gnashes his terrible teeth and cries, "Why are we doing nothing to address climate change!"

"Because there's no such thing," says someone from the White House.

Max turns his boat around, grumbling, "I thought I was supposed to be the one who lived in a fantasy world."

The Very Hungry Syrian Refugee Child

A Syrian refugee child eats an apple on Monday, two pears on Tuesday, three plums on Wednesday and four strawberries on Thursday.

Had he been a caterpillar, that probably would have been enough to save him.

Alice in La-La Land

Alice falls down a rabbit hole and finds herself at a Hollywood awards show, where stars in $10,000 gowns profess liberal solidarity with the poor and oppressed while holding little statues—because that worked so well during the 2016 election.

"Surreal," says Alice.

The Little Legislature That Couldn't

Republicans in Congress, who once condemned candidate Donald Trump for his extreme positions, watch in alarm as President Donald Trump begins to hastily enact them.

"Can we challenge him?" a few ask.

"We think we can; we think we can," the rest answer.

But a few nasty tweets from Trump change their minds, so they give up. The end.

PRESIDENT HAUNTED BY JOB ADVICE IN SPIRITED TALE

Jan 24, 2017

Today I present *Evenings With Trump: A Ghost Story.*

In the nights following his inauguration, Donald Trump was visited by the ghosts of former presidents.

George Washington came first, repeating advice he had given in his farewell address: avoid hyper-partisanship, excessive debt and foreign influence.

Trump was silent for a moment, as if contemplating Washington's words, then said: "How'd you get your picture on the money? I'd like to get my picture on the 1 million dollar bill."

"Did I mention that humility is also an important quality in a leader?" Washington asked.

"I'm the most humble person in the entire world, believe me," Trump replied. "No. 1."

A few days later, Abraham Lincoln stopped by to counsel magnanimity, citing the words inscribed on the Lincoln Memorial: "With malice toward none, with charity for all."

Trump interrupted to ask who sculpted the marble figure at the Lincoln Memorial. "I want one like that, except bigger and with gold leaf. It'll drive the losers crazy."

"I can't look at that memorial," Lincoln observed, "without thinking about the high price a divided nation paid in blood while I was in office."

"So you paid too much?" Trump said. "Well, don't worry: I make great deals."

The visits continued.

Thomas Jefferson urged Trump to resist authoritarian impulses. James Madison advised reading the Bill of Rights. Chester A. Arthur said, "You should grow some sideburns to go with that hair."

Trump began to complain about the chatty chief executives (except for Calvin Coolidge, who didn't say much).

"What do they know, anyway?" Trump groused. "I've got more Twitter followers than all of them combined."

Still, the presidents kept visiting: Andrew Jackson, Ulysses Grant, Grover Cleveland (twice on nonconsecutive nights).

Herbert Hoover noted sadly that history had reduced him to a caricature.

"I'm too smart for that to happen to me," Trump declared, half-listening as he angrily tweeted Alec Baldwin.

Harry Truman told Trump that momentous decisions would be the toughest part of the job. Richard Nixon warned against nursing grudges. Ronald Reagan said his experience with the Soviet Union suggests that former KGB agents are not to be trusted.

Trump, though, was impressed only by the bravado of Theodore Roosevelt, who galloped in on a horse.

"You're the one who said, 'Speak softly and carry a big stick,'" Trump said.

"In your case," Roosevelt replied, "let's amend that to 'Speak softly, tweet rarely and give Mike Pence the big stick.' We might all sleep better."

Finally, one night Bill Clinton wandered in.

A surprised Trump said: "Wait a minute, you're not a ghost. You're not even dead."

"I just had to come see for myself," Clinton said. "Are you sure Hillary isn't living here?"

TRAGEDY IN ORLANDO DISTILLED IN NOVEL WAY

June 16, 2016

I'm working on a dystopian novel, but I'm afraid the plot might be unbelievable.

The title is *Paralyzed Nation.*

See whether it sounds remotely plausible:

In 2016, the ironically named United States of America is divided by strife and mistrust.

Having access to an endless stream of information has somehow made citizens less informed. Free to choose their sources, they gravitate toward the ones that echo what they already believe.

People disagree not just on matters of opinion but on reality itself. Easily provable facts such as where the president was born or whether vaccines are beneficial become the subject of pointless argument.

Social-media lynch mobs, ranting commentators and grandstanding politicians dominate the national conversation. People increasingly segregate themselves by income and political outlook.

Congress operates on a system of legalized bribery that masquerades as "campaign finance." Lawmakers openly beg for money from billionaires, corporations and special-interest groups that expect something in return.

A presidential campaign—pitting a comically intemperate reality TV star against a chronically secretive former secretary of state—simply ratchets the fevered rhetoric to higher levels.

Because the government is too divided to govern, urgent matters go unaddressed. Diseases fester. Poverty worsens. Environmental catastrophes afflict communities long neglected by the people elected to serve them.

Worst of all is the violence.

It plagues urban neighborhoods on a nightly basis. But it can also strike in terrifyingly random locations. People afflicted by mental illness, twisted by extremism or motivated by incomprehensible hatred routinely slaughter innocents in classrooms, offices and theaters with high-powered weapons.

The nation wants to stop such atrocities but can't agree on how.

One faction sees tyranny in any plan to restrict gun ownership, even to people on terrorist watch-lists. Another sees a nation awash in guns as a form of tyranny itself.

Officeholders content themselves with sending pathetic tweets of sympathy after every bloodbath, as if they were elected to a body of morticians.

Then, the worst mass shooting in American history occurs when a man pledging allegiance to the Islamic State terror group kills 49 people and wounds 53 at a gay nightclub.

The hateful act finally unifies the nation in horror—for about five minutes.

Then it's back to accusations as usual: Blame Muslims; blame Obama; blame Republicans; blame Democrats. Ridiculous debates about semantics swirl through the media. Internet commenters insult one another with glee.

In the end, the nation is simply too paralyzed by its own differences to take action.

Lacking any explicit agreement, it settles for an implicit one: Let's all just retreat to our own realities and await the next slaughter.

So that's the plot. I told you it was unbelievable.

NOT EVERY CONGRESS CAN TAKE A LONG BREAK

Aug. 5, 2014

Congress is on vacation?

The U.S. Congress? The one that is supposed to be the chief legislative body of a nation of 318 million people in a time of global upheaval, environmental peril and economic uncertainty?

The one that has obstructed, grandstanded, subpoenaed and fearmongered its way to a dismal record of accomplishment?

Yep, that one.

Did you think I meant the World Potato Congress?

Heavens, no. In fact, I called the World Potato Congress to see whether it, too, is on a five-week vacation.

No, it isn't, general manager John Coady said. After all, it has a big job.

"Our objective is the development and promotion of the potato globally," he said from his office in Canada.

That's right: An organization dedicated to the advancement of a root vegetable can't spare five weeks.

But the key governing body of the most powerful nation, facing probably the most challenging set of problems in human history? Out of the office until further notice.

You won't see the International Congress of Oral Implantologists behaving that way.

"We're still functioning," Ada Feliciano said from its offices in New Jersey. "We're still here."

Well, of course they are.

The International Congress of Oral Implantologists is the world's largest provider of continuing implant education. You don't just walk away from that type of a job for five weeks, leaving an implant-education vacuum.

So, once again, let's review:

Organization dedicated to the placement of artificial teeth into a patient's jawbone? On duty.

Organization that oversees a nuclear arsenal, $3 trillion in spending and the complex infrastructure vital to the prosperity of a 21st-century nation? Kicking back for weeks.

I could understand that behavior better if the job of the U.S. Congress were, say, "to provide standardized rules, regulations and benefits to make bowling fair and fun for everyone."

But, in fact, that is the job of the U.S. Bowling Congress. And guess what? It isn't on vacation, either.

"We're the national governing body for the sport," spokesman Chris Perry said.

Next year, the bowling group will oversee three big tournaments and several smaller ones. It has no time to waste.

I know what you're thinking: Please, please, please can the U.S. Congress and the U.S. Bowling Congress trade jobs?

I'm afraid that the cost would be too high. No doubt, the country would be better off.

The damage to bowling, though, would be awful.

AMERICA IS CHANGING ITS TUNE

July 2, 2013

I decided to rewrite some old songs in light of recent U.S. Supreme Court rulings.

When even Justice Antonin Scalia, in a grumpy dissent, concedes that same-sex marriage throughout the nation seems inevitable, it's time to set things to music.

To review: The court last week struck down the federal Defense of Marriage Act, which defined marriage as the union of one man and one woman.

It also chose not to rule on California's Proposition 8, a ban on same-sex marriage that a lower court had overturned. The next day, same-sex marriages resumed in California.

But enough legalities. Let's get to the songs:

"Same-Sex Marriage"

(*to the tune of the Frank Sinatra hit "Love and Marriage"*)

Same-sex marriage
Same-sex marriage
Scalia lying 'neath its undercarriage
He was squashed by something
Stronger than old men harrumphing.
Same-sex marriage
Same-sex marriage
It's a barrier that some states dare bridge
Now let's add Nebraska,
Ohio, Utah and Alaska.
Try, try, try, Ohio guys,
To picture your tuxedos
As you say your wedding vows

In Dayton or Toledo.
Same-sex marriage
Traditional marriage
They'll be equal, and, though some disparage,
The courts are saying, brother,
You can't have one without the other.

"Get Them to the Church on Time"
(*from* My Fair Lady)

They're getting married in the morning
Ding-dong, the bells are gonna chime
Jill's wedding Mary
And Tom's wedding Harry
So get them to the church on time.
They're gonna be there in the morning
10 o'clock sharp Pacific time
Prop 8's a goner
Thank you, your honor
Now get them to the church on time.
Not just in 'Frisco can they be wed
But in Modesto, Irvine and Merced.
So they're getting married in the morning
No legal hurdles left to climb
Tell Bert and Ernie
They need no attorney
And get them to the church on time.

"At Last"
(*to the Etta James hit "At Last"*)

At last
My love has filed a brief
That devastated DOMA
And left Fox News in grief.
At last
Internal Revenue
Says take the same deduction
That Mr. and Mrs. do.

Soon the right wing might accept us
At potlucks or at the Laundromat
An urge to raise families has swept us
What's more conservative than that?
We smile
Because the die is cast
We'll leave the 19th century
Slowly but at last.

RICHARD III RETURNS BUT HE'S LIVING ON BARD TIME

Feb. 10, 2013

You've no doubt heard that the bones of King Richard III have been found under a parking lot in Britain.

The monarch, dead since 1485, inspired *Richard III,* the Shakespeare play that depicts him as a ruthless, hunchbacked ruler famous for saying, in a moment of battlefield desperation: "A horse! A horse! My kingdom for a horse!"

Well, I think the discovery of his skeleton demands a Shakespeare play of its own, with a few borrowings from other works of the Bard. Because it's kind of a sequel to the original, let's call it *Richard III II: Parking Is Such Sweet Sorrow.*

The play opens with the main character, the skeleton of Richard, alive but lamenting that he faces another year in a cramped grave beneath a parking space—specifically, Row 2, Space B.

RICHARD: Now is the winter of our discontent, when road salt dripping off Toyotas seepeth into my bones. What foul substance be next? Barbecue sauce to make me feel like a buffalo chicken wing?

Suddenly, the sound of jackhammering interrupts his soliloquy.

RICHARD: Hark! What noise from yonder parking lot breaks?

Daylight floods into the grave and excited voices are heard.

EXCAVATOR: Look, a skeleton! With a deformed spine! Could it be?

RICHARD: Yes, it is I, Richard III.

The excavators gasp in amazement.

EXCAVATOR: You talk, yet you are just a skeleton!

RICHARD: Just call it my lean and hungry look. Now take me to a chiropractor. My back is killing me.

Richard the skeleton quickly becomes a sensation in Britain, where he is seen as an amusing offshoot of the zombie craze.

Spending five centuries underground has done nothing to dim his ambitions. He uses his celebrity to arrange a meeting with members of the royal family so he can size them up. Later, he tells his entourage that the royals strike him as pushovers—weak, stuffy and boring.

RICHARD: Methinks it may have been the first time in history that a skeleton entering a room actually enlivened it.

Richard is soon plotting to imprison the royal family in the Tower of London and seize the throne. But he finds that maneuvering secretly is almost impossible because the media follow him everywhere.

RICHARD: I know that all the world's a stage, but this is ridiculous. A villain needs his privacy.

Mindful of what happened the last time he went into battle, Richard makes sure he has extra horses when he sets off with a small band of swordsmen to depose the queen. They advance about a quarter-mile before encountering British artillery, fighter jets and Prince Harry himself in an attack helicopter.

RICHARD: If I might amend an earlier statement: My kingdom for an air force.

Richard is convicted of treason and given a choice: death or 500 more years under Row 2, Space B, in the lot where he was found.

The play ends with him weighing his choice: 2B or not 2B . . .

POPE WALKS A MILE IN ARMANI DRESS SHOES

Sept. 27, 2015

The defense of the status quo is the job of people who hold worldly power.

A spiritual leader's job is to call us to a higher ideal.

Pope Francis did just that in his visit to the United States. It made capitalists, conservatives and climate-change deniers nervous. They don't like hearing their free-market orthodoxy questioned.

As a thought experiment, I tried writing a Francis-style address that defends the economic status quo. He would never do that, but let's just see how inspiring it is:

Dear friends,

How good it is to be with you at this beautiful country club, where you humbly gather to contemplate the many blessings you have bestowed on this suffering world with your financial acumen.

I represent a faith that believes that God himself came to Earth in the form of a poor child. He lived among the poor, served the poor and spoke for the poor. He commanded us to be servants to the poor, saying that the last shall be first and the first, last.

And so today I come to thank you for taking these matters so seriously.

You have done your best to hold down wages, resist environmental regulation and use your considerable influence with politicians to gain favorable tax treatment—but always with the poor utmost in your minds.

For how much worse off would the barista, the dishwasher or the salesclerk be if a reduction in profits meant you could no longer employ them at minimum wage?

The very workers at this club—whom you treat with such kindness when you ask them to bring you a single malt scotch or fetch the Mercedes—have surely grown in compassion for the poor through your example.

As you know, I have expressed great concern about the state of Mother Earth. She groans under the weight of the demands we put on her.

Global warming, habitat destruction, and air and water pollution threaten us all, but they fall most heavily on the vulnerable.

Yet I know that even those of you in the fossil-fuel industry understand and share my concern.

The 30-second commercial in which the members of that nice farm family explain why they allowed fracking on their land has convinced me of your sincerity.

I pray that someday the poor and dispossessed all over the world will see the commercial and rest secure in the knowledge that, even as rising seas lap gently at their hovels, the rich and powerful of the world care about them.

I am not an economist, just a humble servant of God who desires to see all of God's children treated with dignity.

And so I say to all of you: Just keep doing exactly what you're doing. I'm sure that it will all work out.

IT'S TIME WE TRULY PUT KIDS FIRST

Dec. 18, 2012

We tell ourselves a lot of lies in this country, but certainly the biggest one is that we put kids first.

A country that puts children first doesn't run up an enormous debt that those kids will someday pay for—both through taxes and diminished lifestyles.

Nor does it blithely allow more than 20 percent of children to live in poverty.

And, at a bare minimum, it doesn't react to countless school shootings by wringing its hands, lighting a few candles and going about its business.

Maybe that's about to change. Maybe.

"Surely, we can do better," President Obama said on Sunday night in Newtown, Conn.

He was speaking to a town mourning the murders of 20 first-graders and seven adults in a slaughter that I want to say is beyond comprehension except that it's not.

After Columbine High School, Virginia Tech, Aurora, Chardon and other mass shootings too numerous to mention, what could be incomprehensible? We sell weapons in this country expressly designed for mass killing, and we have a few people, for whatever twisted reasons, willing to carry out such crimes.

The suicidal gunman, dressed in dark colors and carrying a 30-shot magazine, is practically an archetype in American life. The only thing incomprehensible is that what we like to call the greatest nation on Earth has taken so long to rouse itself to action.

We all have our biases in this debate. Mine is that I favor gun control. So it would be emotionally satisfying for me to see more of it.

But this isn't about emotional satisfaction. It's about the protection of children.

So we have a choice: We can all retreat to our usual political positions; spend a few months calling one another idiots; and end up, at best, with symbolic legislation that pretends to address the problem.

Or we can shelve our biases and put our considerable resources into figuring out what might actually curb such massacres.

I hope that's what Obama meant when he said, "In the coming weeks, I will use whatever power this office holds to engage my fellow citizens . . . in an effort aimed at preventing more tragedies like this."

One thing we know for sure: This parade of horrors won't stop on its own.

The day after the Connecticut shooting, a man fired 50 shots in a mall parking lot in California.

Today or next week or next month, another such occurrence will happen somewhere else.

Given the dysfunction of Washington, a comprehensive solution might seem a long shot. But I'm hoping that decency or shame or the threat of losing their jobs will move our leaders to cooperate.

Otherwise, we're sending an awful message to the kids we "put first."

Here it is:

> Sorry, kids, but not enough of you have died yet. We're going to wait for another slaughter or two before behaving like the adults we allege to be. Hope you understand.

MODEST PROPOSALS

HOW TO AVOID TOPICAL HEAT ON THE HOLIDAY

Nov. 24, 2016

I'm here to solve the raging Thanksgiving dilemma that faces many families: how to have a peaceful holiday dinner in a divided nation.

Fortunately, it's simple: Avoid politics, and stick to a few safe subjects that lend themselves to pleasant conversation, especially in the swing state of Ohio.

I made a helpful list:

The weather

You can always rely on this classic small-talk topic.

On second thought, maybe you can't.

If it's cold, your climate change-denying relatives are going to cite it as conclusive proof that we are not heating the planet like a microwaved potato. If it's warm, your tree-hugging relatives are going to say it further demonstrates why we must lower our carbon footprints by moving into sod houses and subsisting on moss and insect larvae.

Perhaps it would be best to avoid the weather.

Note: It might be safe to talk about microclimates, as in, "Is it hot in here, or is it just me?"

Sports

It's the perfect . . . wait, no it isn't.

I forgot about the strong opinions provoked by athletes kneeling in protest during the national anthem. So avoid the pregame ceremonies if you're watching football.

In fact, don't even watch football.

I forgot about the concussion issue, which might start an argument over whether the sport is a brutal pastime championed by ruthless capitalists or a character-building pursuit under assault by nanny-state meddlers.

Avoid soccer, too, because it's more popular in blue states than red states. And table tennis, which is dominated by China, which might lead to an argument about the Trans-Pacific Partnership.

Competitive juggling might be OK.

Food

Everyone likes food. Surely, we can all bond over mashed potatoes.

Then again, some minefields exist.

A vegan locavore cousin might insist on organic potatoes grown within 100 feet of the house. That would surely trigger ridicule from a free-market omnivore uncle who buys whatever is on sale at Walmart.

Turkeys can also be highly divisive.

A rugged individualist visiting from Bucyrus might see nothing wrong with a hormone-laden, factory-farmed bird that an animal-rights activist visiting from Yellow Springs regards as an 18-pound sack of toxins and unrealized potential.

You know what?

If you have to talk food, stick to neutral statements about the salt shaker.

Sinuses

OK, I'm pretty sure on this one.

Other states have spring, summer, fall and winter. Ohio has two seasons: allergy and upper-respiratory infection.

Everyone's sinuses are in a constant uproar. The most die-hard liberal and rock-ribbed conservative can see nose-to-nose on the subject.

Yes, I'm saying that mucus is the last safe topic in our swing state.

Let us give thanks for it.

GRADUATES, IT'S TIME TO GET REAL

May 22, 2012

My commencement speech (undelivered) to the college graduates of 2012:

Graduates, if you could put down your smartphones for a moment, I promise this won't take long.

I know you don't want to hear the standard commencement-speech clichés about following your dreams and rising to the challenges of the future.

But your parents do.

After years of paying for your braces, your prom gowns and your educations, they are weary and bankrupt people eager for a note of hope. They want to leave here thinking that you have been sufficiently inspired to go out, establish careers, solve world problems and—most significant—have babies. (It's always about the babies.)

So let's get the part they're eager to hear out of the way: Blah, blah, blah, the future, blah, blah, blah, take risks, blah, blah, blah, follow your passions, blah, blah, blah, find balance, blah, blah, blah, make a difference.

See? Was that so hard? We're almost done.

Oh, but there is one other thing: I want to put in a good word for reality.

You might find this difficult to believe, but it was once taken for granted that everyone accepted reality. People might argue over what to do about reality, but they didn't just go out and make up their own versions of it.

Then came the "information" explosion. I would have sworn that, if you give people more ways to get information, they would come away, you know, informed. Instead, they just pick out the myths, conspiracy theories and facts they like most, mix them together and fashion a reality of their choosing.

Needless to say, this is not a promising basis for problem solving.

The higher the elective office, the less the chance that the people running for it will be dealing in reality.

That is why it's possible for two presidential candidates to propose competing economic plans, neither of which respects the laws of mathematics.

Doesn't this seem the opposite of how things should be? I think all of us have enough generosity of spirit to allow, say, a candidate for township trustee to engage in a few flights of fantasy. When you get to the level of the presidency, though, I think we have to be a little more demanding. Math competence would seem a minimum standard.

Therefore, I call on your generation to be the one that recommits the nation to reality.

Start with something big and observable with the naked eye—such as the polar ice caps. Do they seem to be melting? If so, can everyone agree that this might warrant a rational assessment of the situation before Greenland is submerged? Just asking.

I don't claim that the job will be easy, graduates. People become highly attached to their personal realities.

But, if a previous generation could put a man on the moon, your generation can surely lead us one by one back to reality. Just don't start with the people who claim that the moon landing never happened.

LET'S CREATE WEBSITES THAT REDUCE CONNECTIONS

April 3, 2011

The media have had no new Apple product to worship for several days now, so we've had to turn to other tech news.

"Facebook depression" and a site that facilitates collegiate sexual encounters were among the recent stories.

It turns out that school-age social life can be just as demoralizing online as it is in the real world. Hence, Facebook depression supposedly strikes young people who think they come up short in the "friends" or "status update" department.

Meanwhile, some enterprising students have formed eduHookups.com, a site dedicated to arranging casual sexual encounters between students at Chicago-area colleges. (As Jay Leno observed, we already have something that sparks casual sex between college students. It's called college.)

I bring this up because I think what the world might need about now is anti-social networking.

I know that many people thrive on the constant connection that social networking offers, but others, including me, find it a bit exhausting. Yet we deserve online lives every bit as much as those social e-butterflies with the 5,000 connections on LinkedIn.

For us, I propose new services that will hold the online world at bay. Here are a few:

Avoidpeoplefromelementaryschool.com

Through a sophisticated filter, the site connects only people who didn't know one another before adulthood. It eliminates the possibility of being contacted by someone whose memory of you stops with the recollection that you wet your pants in the second grade.

In moments of insecurity, I can find myself thinking that I haven't progressed beyond age 7. The last thing I need is to hear from people eager to confirm it.

Pontificator

It's the polar opposite of Twitter, the message system with the 140-character limit on tweets. Instead of a character limit, Pontificator has a character minimum: 100,000. Also, footnotes and a bibliography are required with each message ("ponts," to use the jargon).

Obviously, this limits communication to those people who are genuinely interested in your thoughts. Why would you want to hear from anyone else?

eStrife

Find people who are wrong for you on this site. Perhaps you will learn something about relationships. If nothing else, it will make solitude seem more attractive.

Unlinked

If trends continue on LinkedIn, the career-networking site, it won't be long until everyone in the nation is linked to everyone else.

Then what? We'll need another service that cuts ties of dubious value to keep the web of connections meaningful.

That's where Unlinked comes in. Start severing ties now and be ahead of the curve.

Squelch

This is the site for people who like to keep their opinions to themselves. It's like Yelp, except you don't say anything.

FIERY BOLT FROM ABOVE INSPIRES RELIGIOUS THEORIES

June 10, 2010

Most people are ruling out divine intervention in the burning of Ohio's big Jesus, but I'm not ready to move on just yet.

I'm not saying I believe that a message lurked behind the bolt that burned King of Kings, the landmark statue that stood along I-75 between Dayton and Cincinnati.

I'm saying that maybe we haven't fully explored all possible motives. Here are a few I've been contemplating:

God found it too short.

Shockingly, at 65 feet, Ohio's Jesus was comparatively puny for a religious statue.

The Spring Temple Buddha, a Chinese statue called the tallest in the world by an authority on structure heights, is more than 500 feet tall.

King of Kings wasn't even the tallest Jesus. That honor goes to Cristo de la Concordia, a Bolivian giant of 132 feet or so, counting the pedestal.

Nor was it the biggest Jesus in the United States: Christ of the Ozarks, in Arkansas, is usually pegged at 67 feet.

Ohioans thought King of Kings an imposing sight, but one could speculate that God, with a broader perspective, was offended by its insignificance.

Consider: Asia fairly bristles with much taller Buddhas, none of them as yet knocked down by lightning. Of course, this raises the possibility that God is a Buddhist—a tangled proposition I'll leave for theologians to ponder.

God is an art critic.

Let's face it: Big Jesuses are not universally praised for their aesthetic appeal.

Christ of the Ozarks is sometimes called Gumby Jesus for its stiff posture and boxy robes.

King of Kings, with its upraised arms, was often called Touchdown Jesus. Heywood Banks, a comedian, wrote a song that dubbed it Big Butter Jesus because it reminded him of state-fair dairy art.

I thought of it as Poseidon Jesus because the statue's muscular form and pond-side location made me think of the Greek god rising from the sea.

Perhaps the lightning bolt was simply the divine version of a negative review.

God dislikes Big Oil.

King of Kings was largely made of Styrofoam, a petroleum product. That's why it went up in flames so fast.

Perhaps it's no coincidence that this petro-deity got zapped even as oil from a badly drilled well was flowing uncontrollably into the Gulf of Mexico.

Having recklessly unleashed the oily disaster, humans can't do much more than run around in little circles, shrieking like toddlers who scared themselves by turning on the vacuum cleaner.

I could see how this might displease God.

God thought it was wasteful.

I hate to advance this idea because it raises the possibility that countless monuments, steeples, minarets, bell towers and pagodas are in the same category.

One person's frivolous expense is another's sacred symbol, after all.

Certainly, the statue's owners aren't buying it. They vow to rebuild the $250,000 piece.

I'll bet they include a lightning rod.

HE THINKS WE NEED EDGY VEGGIES

Aug. 3, 2006

I think we can all agree on the need for new vegetables.

The old lineup is tired, worn-out, unimaginative.

Fashion changes constantly, and new car models come out once a year. Yet every August, the fields yield the same old array of ripening produce: green beans, squash, eggplant.

How 19th century.

Where's the zest for genetic experimentation that, in other fields, has brought us the Labradoodle puppy and "Pork: The Other White Meat"?

Giving the matter deep thought, So To Speak has devised a list of new, improved vegetables.

They could be coming to a grocery near you.

Or I could be out of my gourd.

Choccoli

The chocolate-infused stalks will undoubtedly raise broccoli's low approval ratings among kids. It will be the Froot Loops of the vegetable world.

*Upside: It's a vitamin-packed vegetable with a rich cocoa taste that no kid can resist.

*Downside: Saying that it's good steamed, raw or on a sugar cone might sound a little odd at first.

Cauliflounder

Aimed at the health-food market, this vegetable would combine the anti-oxidants of cauliflower with the omega-3 fatty acids of fish.

*Upside: It protects against disease and tastes good with both cheese sauce and tartar sauce.

*Downside: The strong smell would require an EPA permit before cooking.

Brewcchini

Why has no one thought of caffeinated zucchini before?

With energy drinks and energy bars abounding, it's about time someone came out with an energy vegetable.

Brewcchini could be eaten as is or pureed with espresso, steamed milk and flavored syrup into a delicious zucchiniccino.

*Upside: It would inject a new vitality into the Obetz Zucchinifest.

*Downside: Decaffeinated zucchini sounds even more pointless than decaffeinated coffee.

Kangaroocumber

This lively vegetable, which can leap up to three times its length, will delight kids.

Part of a new category of dynamic vegetables, the kangaroocumber will clear the way for the turn-turn-turnip (a rotating vegetable) and full-twisting-back-spinach.

*Upside: Vegetables that have to be pursued would counter the effects of our sedentary lifestyle.

*Downside: The trend might lead to disparagus, a vegetable that hurls insults.

Bell pepperoni

Two pizza toppings in one—what more needs to be said?

*Upside: Pizza Hut would undoubtedly soon breed one that comes stuffed with a three-cheese blend.

*Downside: It would cause twice the heartburn of regular peppers.

Rutabagel

Instead of a bulbous root vegetable that has to be peeled and sliced, you get a doughnut-shaped delight, perfect for those mornings when you need to grab a quick snack and go.

*Upside: It could come in onion and garlic flavors.

*Downside: It might be some years before anyone develops a presliced variety.

Corn on the curb

Say goodbye to canned kernels once this street corn, bred to thrive in urban environments, makes its debut. Fresh corn will be as close as the grassy strip between sidewalk and street.

*Upside: Gleaming golden kernels could mimic fashionable hip-hop grilles.

*Downside: It still gets stuck in your teeth.

BETTER ELECTIONS JUST NINE RULES AWAY

Oct. 26, 2010

As we near the end of another political campaign season, I'd like to propose nine simple rules for the next time:

Rule 1: Anyone who wants to run for public office will be automatically disqualified from doing so.

The existing process has simply grown too absurd for anyone of sound judgment to participate.

Rule 2: Henceforth, the jury-duty model will be employed for picking candidates: 12 registered voters, chosen by lottery, will run for office.

The 12 will be sent to an island and, as on *Survivor*, face challenges, form alliances and vote one another out until two remain. Those two will promptly be disqualified for being too ambitious to be worthy of the public trust. (See Rule 1.)

The third- and fourth-place finishers will be declared the candidates, running against each other for the office.

Rule 3: No campaign commercial can be shorter than five minutes.

That might sound counterintuitive to the goal of making campaigns less irksome, but consider this: A 30-second commercial is one thing, but sensible candidates wouldn't risk alienating voters by interrupting *Glee* for five full minutes.

Those who would risk it have an inflated sense of their own importance that makes them unfit for office. (See Rule 1.)

Rule 4: Candidates who appear in campaign commercials wearing hard hats and safety glasses must, if elected, wear those items at all times in public for the next four years.

Candidates who appear in ads with their children must bring those children to the office every day for the next four years.

Rule 5: When a campaign has become insufferable, the people can end it by calling for the election immediately.

(The John Kasich-Ted Strickland race for governor would have been over in four days.)

Rule 6: In a two-person race, the voters will be given three options: Candidate A, Candidate B and You Should Both Be Ashamed of Yourselves.

Rule 7: Any person, corporation or shadowy network of anonymous donors can contribute to a political campaign without restriction.

But that same person, corporation or shadowy network of anonymous donors must contribute an equal amount to something that does some good for society.

Rule 8: Every promise to improve the economy must be accompanied by a spreadsheet offering specifics.

If the spreadsheet lacks sufficient detail, the candidate will be stricken from the ballot for pretending he has the ability to control the economy.

If the spreadsheet is too detailed, the candidate will be stricken from the ballot for *believing* he has the ability to control the economy.

Rule 9: Never forget Rule 1.

ABOUT THE AUTHOR

Joe Blundo's column "So To Speak" has been published in the *Columbus Dispatch* since 1997. It's long been a mix of humor, human interest and information. He has won awards from the *Associated Press,* Society of Professional Journalists and the National Society of Newspaper Columnists for his work. Joe, a native of New Castle, Pa., and a graduate of Kent State University, began his journalism career in 1976 at the Parkersburg (W.Va.) *Sentinel* before joining the *Dispatch* in 1978. He lives in Worthington, Ohio, with his wife, Deborah. They have two children and a grandson.